Introducing the Cultural Context of the Old Testament

John J. Pilch, Ph.D.

HEAR THE WORD!
Volume 1

PAULIST PRESS

New York/Mahwah

Published by Paulist Press
997 Macarthur Boulevard
Mahwah, NJ 07430

Printed and bound in the
United States of America

CONTENTS

Introduction

Father Isaac Thomas Hecker (1819–1888), founder of the Paulist Fathers, said: "I have the conviction that I can be all the better Catholic because I am an American; and all the better American because I am Catholic." The Paulist Press is just one of the ministries developed by the followers of Father Hecker to help all American Catholics fulfill that conviction.

Father Hecker's belief anticipated the Second Vatican Council by nearly one hundred years. In their Pastoral Constitution on the Church in the Modern World, the council fathers observed:

> Faithful to her own tradition and at the same time conscious of her universal mission, [the Church] can enter into communion with various cultural modes, to her own enrichment and theirs too. (n. 58)

This is as true of the twentieth-century United States as it is of any contemporary third-world country.

American Catholics should be encouraged to strive for a deeper understanding of their culture and their faith. But such an effort soon discovers that American culture and the culture of our biblical ancestors in the faith are quite different from each other. If the differences between these two cultures are not recognized and respected, the modern American Bible reader unwittingly transforms the persons of the Bible into Americans. Biblical characters begin to look, think, speak and behave like Americans. From this perspective, interpreting the Bible is easy because the English words, phrases and sentences we read in our translations are presumed to mean exactly what we understand by these same words.

Our ancestors, however, spoke different languages (Hebrew, Aramaic, Greek and perhaps others) and lived in a different culture. To be considerate readers and show respect to our ancestors it would be helpful to understand that culture.

This Bible-study program adopts such an approach as a complement to the many fine Bible programs, handbooks, and resources currently available. It will not try to repeat what can be easily found in other reliable sources, but will seek to understand the cultural context in which our ancestors lived.

At the same time, the new challenge resulting from such a study will be the need for a redoubled effort to make appropriate applications to our lives. After all, we are Americans and not Mediterraneans. Our cultures are different. Their problems are not our problems; their solutions might not work for us. This is why the American bishops caution us against trying "to find in the Bible all the direct answers for living."

Bridging our different cultures is possible, but it requires serious study and skilled efforts. This program hopes to assist in every way it can.

Father Hecker also noted:

> So far as it is compatible with faith and piety, I am accepting the American civilization with its usages and customs; leaving aside other reasons, it is the only way by which Catholicity can become the religion of our people. The character and spirit of our people, and of their institutions, must find themselves at home in our Church in the way those of other nations have

done; and it is on this basis alone that the Catholic religion can make progress in our country.

To know American culture well will make us better Americans. To understand the Mediterranean culture of our biblical ancestors in the faith will help us appreciate our Catholic identity. Developing a creative link between the two cultures will help us to realize Father Hecker's dream. It is a dream shared not only by his followers, the Paulists, but one worthy to be shared by all American Catholics as well.

How to Use This Workbook

This workbook is designed for any adult who is interested in a serious and/or scientific study of the Bible. It is a workbook in the sense that few Bible passages are quoted; the reader must find these passages and read them in a Bible. After reading the biblical passage in its context, the reader is invited to write out the full text, or jot down notes, or mark up a personal copy of the Bible and, of course, to answer the questions in this workbook that are keyed to what was just read.

This Bible-study program therefore requires only a few things:

1. A Bible
2. This workbook
3. Sufficient time to read the Bible, use the workbook, and reflect individually or discuss with others.

For those interested in pursuing some of the insights and topics further, other resources are listed. *These are not required as part of this program, nor is it expected that anyone will have the time to consult these resources while studying this program.* The references are provided as an answer to the anticipated question by some participants: "What next?" Or "Where can I read more about this?"

Serious or scientific study of the Bible is not the same as meditating on the Bible, or praying with the Bible, or reading the Bible for pleasure. All of these are legitimate uses of the Bible, and Bible study will contribute to all of them. Serious or scientific study of the Bible is just like any other such study you have already experienced in life, whether the field was business, health care, or learning a craft or skill like typing, playing a musical instrument, or computer processing. A number of things are involved.

1. Time. Serious study takes time. How much time will this study take: an hour? two? more? That depends on many things, such as how much the learner already knows, how fast the learner can search for and find the passages in the Bible, and how quickly any individual can grasp and apply new ideas and strategies. Above all, it depends on how much time is available, or how much time one can make available. Learners, individually and as a group, will have to determine how to arrange the time advantageously.

Under ideal conditions, this program would envisage a couple of hours in preparation, perhaps two or three hours for the lesson itself; and a couple of hours as follow-up. The ideal minimum amount of time for each topic thus would be six hours.

How should the eight topics in each book be studied—over a period of eight weeks or eight months? A group in Memphis, Tennessee using a highly successful adult Bible-study program published by Paulist Press met once a week for eight weeks.

BUT the program expected that the participants had been studying daily for five days, had reviewed and reflected upon that study on the sixth day, and then met on the seventh day in a small group in order to share insights. This is one form of a once-a-week meeting that extends over eight weeks. Obviously, much more time is involved than the formula "two hours once a week for eight weeks" indicates.

This program proposes a similar time commitment. If the learner decides on once a week, that period will gain in value from some preparation and from some follow-up. At an earlier time of life these were called "preparing for class" and "homework," respectively. Anyone who took those activities seriously remembers that they paid rich dividends then. They still can now.

2. Commitment. In the tiny village of Grouard, 230 miles northwest of Edmonton, in the province of Alberta in Canada, a small group of people explored the feasibility of initiating a weekly program of Bible study. Even in this town, activities filled almost every evening and made it difficult for the Bible-study group to select a time convenient for everyone.

However, knowledge of the Bible was a requisite in a Ministry-Formation program, and participants in this Bible-study program each "invested" a significant sum of money to purchase the materials. These two elements (a requirement and an "investment") seemed to strengthen the group members' commitment to the perfect attendance that followed. In fairness it must also be noted that the participants discovered that they actually enjoyed serious study of the Bible. And their joy was so contagious that, within a year, two new groups formed, and the busy village managed to clear Monday nights on the calendar, so that the Bible-study groups could meet without distractions from other events.

Whatever your motive for devoting yourself to serious study of the Bible, strive for strong commitment. This is as important for the lone learner as it is for the learner who is a member of a group. Once the time has been established, resolve not to miss any part of it except for the most serious of reasons.

3. Participation. Like many other programs, the success of this one, too, depends upon participation. Basically, in this program participation means *reading!* The learner must read the Bible and read the workbook. It is imperative to look up all the Bible texts suggested, and to read them in the light of the information and strategies suggested in the workbook.

It is helpful if a learner has at least one partner with whom to discuss and share what is being learned; it is preferable to participate in a small group which allows for the interplay of a variety of talents, experiences and insights. Moreover, with a group it is possible to divide material so that each participant is responsible for some of it, but all will gain as a result of the communal meeting and sharing.

The knowledge gained in this program will not only enhance personal knowledge of the Bible and its Mediterranean cultural context, but will also heighten the learner's awareness of the need for similar cultural sensitivity in comprehending news items reported from around the globe. Understanding and respecting foreign cultures are not strong suits in American culture.

The Method

Each session or chapter in the book contains three parts: Preparation; Lesson; Follow-up.

Preparation. The purpose of the preparation is to stimulate or awaken the desire to learn. A variety of strategies are invoked. Pertinent films available on video-cassette offer unique challenges. Even if the films are unavailable, or time for viewing films is scarce, references are made at least to key scenes as they relate to the lesson at hand. More than 58 percent of homes in the United States have a video-cassette recorder, and practically every institution has one for its educational programs. A good picture is worth a thousand words, and there are many excellent "pictures" that can make the points of this Bible-study program quickly and effectively.

At other times, summaries of research are proposed as a framework for reading texts. Whatever stimulates interest in the topic at hand is acceptable. Alternatives—especially films or other audio-visual aids—discovered by the readers themselves would be welcome additions. Experience indicates that once learners discover an exciting insight, they are able to locate many excellent illustrations of the insight.

Lesson. This is, of course, the heart of the program. This is what the learner is expected to master. It is expected that the learner will read all biblical passages and will explore and analyze them in the cultural context presented. Discussion with others is especially helpful, but a solo learner can also manage well. Even so, don't hesitate to tailor the material to suit the time available.

Follow-up. No amount of time allotted for the lesson is ever enough. It is wise to set limits and to stick with the time limit established. The follow-up suggestions are intended to help the learner utilize some time after the lesson either to continue the lesson, or to "follow-up" its insights with additional explorations or investigations.

Logistically, the learner or the group will have to determine how to arrange time so that the follow-up does not impinge on the preparation for the next session.

The Individual Learner

The person who is unable to join in a group venture can still benefit from this program. Obviously, the major benefit is that the time which might have been spent in discussions and meetings with other learners can now be devoted to reading, especially the Bible.

On the other hand, the disadvantage for the solo learner is the lost opportunity to hear other interpretations and viewpoints as well as the definite loss of enhanced effectiveness and efficient use of scarce time that derives from group collaboration on a common project.

The individual learner, therefore, should seek opportunities for sharing knowledge even in the most informal settings. The opportunity to summarize and report to others what one has learned is a valuable motivating factor for mastering what one is learning. Such sharing might also interest the listener in taking up a similar program of serious Bible study.

Session One

Guidelines for Interpreting the Bible

During the 1988 Presidential campaign, Republican candidate George Bush told the League of United Latin American Citizens in convention that, if elected president, he would appoint a Hispanic to his cabinet. Here are three reports of that announcement:

> "The audience applauded Bush's promise."
> —*The Washington Post*

> "The audience gave the vice president only scattered applause."
> —Associated Press dispatch in
> *The Baltimore Sun*

> "The vice president's promise drew a standing ovation from the several thousand gathered conventioneers."
> —*The New York Times*

If you were not present at that convention, how would you determine which of these three reports—in three different respectable newspapers—best described the event?

Though we take great pride in being able to arrive at the factual truth, "God's honest truth," the fact is that we are bombarded with interpretation, on a regular and routine basis.

The Bible, too, is not "live at five with film at ten (or eleven, depending on the time zone in which you live)." It is, in fact, a book of interpretation which itself requires interpretation.

The focus of this session is biblical interpretation.

Preparation: View *The Gods Must be Crazy*

Lesson: The church's guidelines for interpreting the Bible

Follow-up: View two TV newscasts; CBS, ABC, or NBC

PREPARATION

1. If possible, please view the film *The Gods Must Be Crazy*. The story is situated in southern Africa and features a bushman, Xi, (pronounced "ki") from the Kalahari Desert, an ecologist, Andrew Steyn, along with his native assistant, and Ms. Kate Thompson, a woman from "civilization" who comes to teach in the mission school.

Carefully observe and jot down the beliefs and behaviors of Xi, noting how they differ from your own beliefs and behaviors. For instance, compare Xi's outlook on nature (live in harmony with it) to a modern American outlook (strive to master nature), or his outlook on time (no calendar or clocks) to a modern outlook (ruled by calendars and clocks).

In the scene where Andrew tries to explain to Ms. Kate that a rhinoceros instinctively stamps out fires, and she is reluctant to believe him, do the natives nod their heads *side-to-side* to indicate "yes"? Do we nod our heads *up-and-down* to indicate that same thing? Is this why Ms. Kate totally misunderstood the natives and consequently refused to trust Andrew? This is but one example among hundreds in this film, showing how culture shapes our perception, understanding, interpretation, and spoken as well as body language.

Compare Xi's interpretation of the significance of the coke bottle and his understanding of the "gods" with your interpretations.

The purpose of this film is to prepare the modern Bible reader to be respectful of the "foreigners" who populate the pages of the Bible. Since our ancestors in the faith are not American, we should expect them to be quite different from us in how they perceive, understand, interpret, and speak with language as well as with their bodies. This program of serious Bible study will introduce modern readers to the cultural context of our ancestors in the faith in order to better understand them and the literature they have left us.

2. If it is not possible for you to rent and view this film, please proceed to the next suggestion.

Please read the Vatican II Document on Divine Revelation, especially Chapter III: The Divine Inspiration and the Interpretation of Sacred Scripture. Study carefully paragraph n. 12. Read also the 1987 U.S. Bishops' Pastoral Statement for Catholics on Biblical Fundamentalism. Underline or jot down the statements that catch your attention.

LESSON: Guidelines for Interpretation

Listen to three baseball umpires describe their job:

1. "I call them as they are."
2. "They're nothing 'till I call them."
3. "I call them as I see them."

These three statements reflect three different views of reality. The first umpire believes that reality is totally objective. The baseball as it comes toward home plate, even if no one is looking at it, would be a "ball" or a "strike." The second umpire believes that reality is totally subjective: that is, reality is entirely constructed by the human person. The third umpire sees value in both positions and tries to balance both; the baseball could be "objectively" in its proper zone, or outside of it, but the call will depend upon the "subjective" judgment (the eyesight, angle of vision, etc.) of the umpire.

Some Bible readers choose to believe that the Bible is objectively factual, word-for-word, and prefer to interpret everything as it is, because they believe the biblical interpreter is like the first umpire—the authors literally report what factually occurred. Interpreters "tell it like it is"; that is, as they read and understand it (in English, of course!).

Other Bible readers believe that the biblical interpreter creates reality like the second umpire creates balls and strikes. The events are there but it is the creativity of the biblical interpreter that finds or puts meaning into the events and then composes a suitable interpretation to make the point. Often one hears such interpreters claim that "once it leaves the author's pen (or quill), the text has a life of its own." For the modern believer who views the role of a biblical interpreter in this way, these naive and primitive stories and reports of the Bible clamor to be radically reinterpreted.

Finally, some Bible readers believe that the interpreters and the sacred authors were dealing with objective reality in a subjective way. Events took place: some people perceived a special significance in these events, while others did not. The biblical author strives mightily to report the significance of these events, and biblical interpreters strive mightily to discover what the author intended to communicate.

This last case is the one that best describes the church's understanding of biblical authors and their interpreters.

Vatican II Document on Revelation

The Vatican II Document on Divine Revelation (especially Chapter III, paragraphs 11 and 12) offers these stirring reflections:

1. "In composing the sacred books, God chose [human beings] and while employed by Him they made use of their powers and abilities, so that with Him acting in them and through them, they as true authors, consigned to writing everything and only those things which He wanted." (n. 11)

   a. God chose human beings to compose the sacred books.

   READ the Foreword or Prologue to the book of Sirach (Ecclesiasticus). What can you learn from this about the human being or beings involved in writing and translating this book?

   b. What "powers and abilities" does a person need to be an author—keen eyesight? sharp hearing? tenacious memory? huge vocabulary? ability to write?

ability to compose? ability to tell a story? ability to create a story? mastery of language?

What else would you include in your list?

What powers and abilities does the author of Sirach manifest?

As you study the different books of the Bible, keep these qualifications in mind.

2. "God speaks in sacred Scripture through [human beings] in human fashion." (n. 12)

What is a "human fashion" of speaking?

– What human language or languages are involved?

– Is the language concrete or abstract or mixed?

– Is it high-class, low-class, no class (i.e., class-free)?

– Does God speak in prose or in poetry?

– Is the communication clear or muddled?

Some scholars advise Bible readers to pay attention to (1) style, (2) vocabulary, and (3) viewpoint as they read a book or portions of a book.

READ Ecclesiastes 1 and Song of Songs 1. Can you identify differences of style, vocabulary, and viewpoint between the authors of these two books? Is this what "human fashion" of speaking might mean?

3. "The interpreter of sacred Scripture, in order to see clearly what God wanted to communicate to us, should carefully investigate what meaning the sacred writer really intended, and what God wanted to manifest by means of their words." (n. 12)

a. How does one investigate "what meaning the sacred writer really intended"?

READ Proverbs 1:1–7 and discuss what the sacred writer really intended here.

b. How does one know that one has discovered "what God wanted to manifest by means of their words"?

READ Proverbs 6:20–35.

– What did the sacred writer intend and what did God want to manifest by the discussion in verses 30–35?

– Is adultery considered just a different form of stealing (compare verses 31 and 34–35)?

– Is the thief OK as long as he doesn't get caught (vv 30–31)?

c. Where would you look for help in this challenge from Vatican II?

4. "Those who search out the intention of the sacred writers must, among other things, have regard for *literary forms.*"

Here is one way suggested by the council fathers by which we can try to discover what the author intended to say and what God wanted to manifest.

How does a junk-mail letter differ from a personal letter? This reflection will help you understand literary forms. A junk-mail letter and a personal letter are both letters. But junk-mail letters will never be signed "Love, your local grocery store." What other differences in "form" can you think of between these two kinds of letters?

The council fathers single out some common literary forms in the Bible: "history of one kind or another," "prophecy, poetry, or some other type of speech." Here are some hints to help you find examples of these forms in your Old Testament.

a. History of one kind or another:

• COMPARE 2 Samuel 24 and 1 Chronicles 21.

Who inspired David to take a census?

Why are there two different answers to this question?

Which answer makes David look good?

Which answer makes David look bad?

Do these books (Samuel and Chronicles) represent two different kinds of "history"?

• COMPARE 2 Samuel 11 and 1 Chronicles 20.

What happened to Bathsheba in Chronicles?

She is so central to the story in Samuel. How can she just disappear or be ignored in Chronicles?

Relative to the Bathsheba incident, does Chronicles seem to "whitewash" David's life-story?

• READ Sirach 47 on King David. How does it compare with 2 Samuel and 1 Chronicles?

1–2 Samuel, 1–2 Chronicles, and Sirach 44–49 are three different kinds of history, concerning essentially the same events. We will return to a consideration of "history" in session seven of this book.

At this point the reader is encouraged to simply note the variety of interpretations given to the same persons and events in different parts of the Bible.

b. Prophecy:

> • READ any of the prophets, e.g., Amos 1:3–5; 1:6–8.

> What does the "literary form" of a prophetic speech look like?

> How does it usually begin?

> Is the message good news or bad news?

> Is there a discernible pattern?

c. Poetry:

> • READ some Psalms.

> Do verses sometimes seem repetitious?

> Do they offer contrasts?

> Do verses rhyme?

> What have you observed about poetry in the Bible?

5. "The interpreter must investigate what meaning the sacred writer *intended to express and actually expressed* in particular circumstances . . . [as he used literary forms according to] his own time and culture."

> How can we distinguish between what an author "intended to express and actually expressed"?

READ Jeremiah 13. Is this a lesson in garment care, or a message from the Lord?

6. "Due attention must be paid to the customary and characteristic *style of perceiving, speaking, and narrating* which prevailed at the time of the sacred writer, and to the *customs* [human beings] normally followed at that period in their everyday dealings with one another."

Most of the books published in the last twenty to twenty-five years have dealt extensively with styles of "narrating." The "literary forms" introduced immediately above are examples of styles of narration.

Fewer studies have dealt with styles of *speaking* and still fewer with styles of *perceiving.* Those who study speaking styles point out evidence in the text that the scriptures (a word that literally means "something written") were originally spoken. They call this feature "orality." For instance, Psalm 136 repeats a refrain: "For His loving kindness endures forever." It is easy to imagine the setting: a chorus invites the congregation to give thanks to the Lord for many things, and the congregation responds with the same refrain in what we might call a litany style. The congregation didn't need a songbook to participate in this "Great Hallel."

Scholarship of nearly two decades now has also been focusing on the style of *perceiving.* Perception is shaped by culture. For instance, the Hopi Indian language has only two words for colors. As a result, Hopi Indians perceive reality in two colors. If this sounds strange, on your next visit to the paint section in the hardware store notice how many kinds of white paint are available. One brand features twelve varieties of "whites and whisper whites." If you do not have any other "white" with which to compare the particular "white" you are viewing, would you be able to identify it by the precise name? To make matters even more complex, pick up the white paint shades available in another brand and notice that comparable, if not exact, shades of "white" do not carry the same name across brands. This is just one example of a style of perceiving.

Consider another example illustrating styles of perception as well as *custom*. In the United States, we think nothing of entering a public meeting room and sitting wherever we like. From the front of the room, one will see men and women intermingled whether related or not. Our Mediterranean ancestors in the faith would have been scandalized. If you have ever travelled in Greece or visited the Greek neighborhood of your city, you may have seen coffee houses. Have you ever noticed the absence of women in these places? Many cultures perceive the world and all reality as divided into masculine and feminine segments.

Some places (a coffee house) are masculine and women are excluded, while others (a kitchen) are feminine and men are excluded. Some places (like the public square) are both masculine and feminine, and men and women are allowed there but not at the same time. Women are permitted in the square in the morning, and men in the afternoon. Jesus meets the Samaritan woman at the well at noon (John 4). Who is out of place?

Even when men and women can be in the same location, as in an Orthodox Church or Orthodox synagogue, they must keep themselves separate. This is an example of cultural custom determining how men and women should relate or associate in the Mediterranean area.

This study program will pay special attention to the different styles of perception and cultural customs among our ancestors in the faith. It will strive to broaden understanding of and appreciation for those perceptions, lest Bible readers make the same mistake Ms. Kate made in her misperception of the meaning conveyed by the side-to-side shaking of the head by the Africans, whose language she did not understand in the film *The Gods Must be Crazy*.

U.S. Bishop's Pastoral Statement for Catholics on Biblical Fundamentalism (1987)

READ and discuss this short document with others. The following excerpts from it might stimulate reflection and discussion.

"We do not look upon the Bible as an authority for science or history. We see truth in the Bible as not to be reduced solely to literal truth, but also to include salvation truths expressed in varied literary forms."

> What is "literal truth" and what are "salvation truths"? Can you find examples in your Bible? How would you apply this distinction to Genesis 1–3?

The bishops also caution against "an effort to try to find in the Bible all the direct answers for living," because the Bible itself nowhere claims such authority.

The Bible did not know about nuclear power, atomic bombs, microscopes, telephones, television, and many other things which were invented or discovered centuries later. For this reason, the Bible cannot offer "direct answers" to problems in daily living related to these and other items.

"We (Catholics) look to both the Church's official teaching and Scripture for guidance in addressing life's problems."

> Notice how the bishops point to the documents of Vatican II and other documents as indispensable in coming to grips with life's problems.

"It is important for every Catholic to realize that the Church produced the New Testament, not vice versa. The Bible did not come down from heaven, whole and intact, given by the Holy Spirit. Just as the experience and faith of Israel developed its sacred books, so was the early Christian Church the matrix of the New Testament. …The first generation of Christians had no New Testament at all—but they were the church then, just as we are the church today."

We will return to this document in the NT Introduction and at other times in the program. For now it suffices for the participants to become familiar with it.

Conclusion to the Lesson

Pause to review and summarize the guidelines proposed in this lesson for those who would read and interpret the scriptures with sensitive consideration to their ancestors in the faith.

1. Biblical authors are human beings with normal human powers and abilities. Specifically, biblical authors are Mediterranean personalities who—just like biblical characters—reflect Mediterranean culture, customs, and styles of perceiving, thinking and speaking or writing.

2. Through these human authors God consigned to writing everything and only those things he wanted.

3. To discover what God intended, the reader must consider what the sacred author actually expressed and intended to express.

4. One helpful tool for understanding the sacred author is to understand the literary forms used and appreciated in the culture.

5. Knowing the author's Mediterranean culture helps a reader to determine culturally plausible interpretations. Such knowledge not only improves the chances of identifying the correct interpretation but also mini-

mizes the risk that the reader will impose an alien cultural interpretation upon the Mediterranean text.

FOLLOW-UP

After completing the lesson, be particularly sensitive to interpretations you see and hear in daily life. Here are a few suggestions.

1. If it is possible in your region, watch two national TV newscasts on a given evening. During the first program, jot down the events reported and try to remember what is reported. During the second program, notice which events are repeated and whether the report is identical or different: e.g., more footage of a person's speech, or an event. Notice also if the presentation of similar stories is the same, or if the order of presentation differs. For instance, does the same event lead off each telecast? All of these and other strategies are techniques of interpretation. The news is not simply reported; it is interpreted heavily in the process.

2. On TV newscasts or in the daily newspapers, pay attention to reports on "foreigners." For example, in some areas of the country, the weekly health section of the newspaper may report on a local minority group, perhaps recent immigrants. Are their cultural folk ways respectfully reported, or are they criticized or ridiculed? Are aliens encouraged to become "American," or to preserve their language and heritage? Are their folk therapies explored and understood or dismissed as "mumbo-jumbo" and "superstition"?

3. In the above two examples, or other experiences you can observe, how difficult is it to resist putting unsuitable

interpretations on events or people of other cultures? Do you think American Bible readers ever insert American ways of perceiving, thinking, and speaking into biblical passages? Can you offer some examples?

Looking Ahead

In the following sessions, we will focus on two cultures: mainstream American culture and the Mediterranean culture of antiquity in order to become aware of the differences between them. Respecting these differences will influence our understanding and interpretation of our ancestors. It will also challenge us to be more diligent as we seek relevance in the biblical heritage for our theology, spirituality, and daily life. We will better understand the caution of the U.S. bishops against trying "to find in the Bible all the direct answers for living."

Session Two

Overview of the Wisdom Literature in a Mediterranean Cultural Perspective

The special focus of this program is the Mediterranean culture in which the Bible originated. This culture is such an integral part of the biblical story and message that it cannot be disregarded or set aside in order to focus on some other aspect of the Bible. Rather, this culture colors the Bible's story and message so strongly that it is actually the Bible's *first* interpretation. All other interpretations have to begin with this one.

The best window through which a Bible reader can peek in on this Mediterranean culture is folklore or folk wisdom. This "wisdom" literature is the result of the creative contribution of many generations of people to the heritage of a given culture. For this reason, the present portion of this Bible-study program will focus on the Bible's wisdom literature, especially Proverbs and Sirach.

Preparation: Learn some "tools" that will increase sensitivity to the cultural information contained in the wisdom literature.

Lesson: Take a broad overview of the seven wisdom books in the Bible in order to gain familiarity with this collection. Some Mediterranean

> cultural aspects of each book will be briefly highlighted. Fuller treatment will be presented in other parts of this program.
>
> *Follow-up:* Practice increasing sensitivity to and respect for the cultural differences in the Bible as well as the world around you.

PREPARATION

In a broad sense, culture includes everything people learn to do. Beginning at birth, individuals are trained in the proper rules and models for responding to an endless variety of life situations: eating, sleeping, relating to others (parents, relatives, neighbors, friends, strangers), and so forth. The patterns of behavior an individual learns allow that person to relate to the entire social order of origin. Culture, therefore, is a sum total of life.

As soon as a person becomes aware of or encounters another culture, that person realizes that some people have other ways of responding to these same life situations. While everyone on this planet eats, they eat different foods, observe different rules of etiquette, are allowed or not allowed to eat with certain people, and so on. This and much more is determined by culture.

Here are some tools, or guidelines, to assist a Bible-reader in becoming aware of the distinctive Mediterranean culture of our biblical ancestors in the faith.

1. *Be curious.*

Proverbs 10:26 compares a sluggish messenger to "vinegar to the teeth, and smoke to the eyes." What do you know about vinegar and teeth? What effect does vinegar have on teeth? What kind of vinegar was known in the Mediterranean world? Where did it come from? What do you know of "dental health" in the Mediterranean world? Where could you learn the answers to the questions you raise? How will you satisfy your curiosity?

2. Take note of *culturally conditioned* behavior.

Proverbs 16:30 assigns a certain meaning to "winking the eyes" and "compressing one's lips." Compare this to the description of a worthless person in Proverbs 6:12–15. Have you ever winked at a child? In your culture, what would it mean if a man winked at another man? A man winked at a woman? How does culture suggest or propose certain behaviors, and assign these behaviors meanings?

3. Observe the *cultural connotations* of language.

The word "beautiful" means different things in different languages. In one culture "fat is beautiful, and skinny is ugly," while in another culture "fat is ugly, skinny is beautiful." How would you describe "beautiful" women of Italy, France, Germany, Norway, Iraq, and other countries? Browse through the Song of Songs and see if you can identify how the boy and girl perceive and describe each other's "beauty." Is that different from your idea of beauty? Who said "beauty is in the eye of the beholder"?

4. Pay attention to *social variables* such as age, gender, social class.

Proverbs 31:10–31 describes a "good wife." After reading this passage over, would you conclude that a wife who behaves otherwise, or a married couple who have reversed their roles, might not be described as "good"? Judging by the kinds of things the wife does in this passage, what would you guess her social class might be? In other words, what age, gender, and social class can you dig out of this text?

Sirach 42:9–11 reflects on a woman through various stages of life. How do these stages reveal a changed perspective? What perspective stays the same? Are sons in Proverbs viewed in the same way that this passage views a daughter?

5. Jot down *conventional behavior* that you perceive in commonly recurring situations.

Two proverbs reflect upon a contentious or quarreling wife: 19:13 and 27:15. Would you conclude that a Mediterranean wife is normally expected to be quiet? accommodating? peaceable?

A contentious and quarrelsome woman is compared to "a continual dripping of rain." Where would this dripping rain most bother a person: outdoors or indoors? Very likely indoors.

An Arab proverbs notes:
"Three things make a house uninhabitable:
leakage of rain (*tak*),
a woman's nagging (*nak*),
and bugs (*bak*)."

Proverbs 19:13 which compares a woman's quarreling to a continual dripping rain is followed in 19:14 by reference to *house* and wealth. Would you agree that the common experience behind all these proverbs is a peaceful house, undisturbed by a dripping rain or a quarrelsome wife?

Does this cluster of ideas help you to appreciate the value of becoming sensitive to the cultural context of the Bible?

Conclusion to the Preparation for the Lesson

Five tools, or viewpoints, are proposed as basic travelling baggage for the American or person from any culture who is interested in respecting the culture of the Mediterranean authors and the subjects of the Bible. These tools will help the reader to be sensitive to the cultural clues for proper interpretation of the biblical literature itself. The section of the Bible in which these cultural insights are most readily available is the collection of seven wisdom books. To these the reader is now invited to turn.

LESSON: The Wisdom Books of the Bible

Here is the cluster of seven books in the Bible that are generally described as "wisdom books."

1. Proverbs

2. Sirach, also called Ecclesiasticus

3. Ecclesiastes, also called Qoheleth

4. Job

5. The Wisdom of Solomon

6. The Canticle of Canticles (Song of Songs)

7. Psalms, particularly those called "wisdom psalms."

The single most important characteristic of all these books that explains why they have traditionally been gathered together as a collection is that they maintain an unwavering and concentrated focus on reflecting upon the world from a secular or not-explicitly religious viewpoint throughout.

A good illustration of such a perspective is the patriarch Joseph whose story is narrated in Genesis 37–50. He receives no revelation from God, but he judges and acts wisely, he behaves with discretion and prudence, and he does God's will as he perceives it in the events in which he is involved.

Other characteristics which these books share in common include:

1. an obvious and consistent focus on the *intellectual reflection* about life's problems. Religious traditions like the Torah of Sinai, the covenant, worship, or the special status of Israel do not loom large in these books.

2. a quest for universal truth drawn from the *universal human experiences* shared by *all* people and not

just those who believe in God. Human experience is valued highly.

3. a *questioning attitude* about the problems of life: good and evil, suffering, success and failure, death, the apparently arbitrary and often "undeserved" fate that falls to people, etc.

4. a genuine interest in *how to master life*, and a concern for discovering rules that should govern good living.

5. a deep *curiosity and respect* for creation, nature.

This secular, or not-explicitly religious, or worldly viewpoint is actually a rather clear reflection of the *culture* in which this literature originated, or from which it borrowed. Culture here should be understood as a broad concept that embraces all aspects of human life. Specifically, the wisdom literature in the Bible provides us with a window on the Mediterranean culture of our ancestors in the faith. By peeking in through this window, we can observe various patterns of living reflected and recorded there. The wisdom books of the Bible help us grasp an individual's role in the unending varieties of life settings of all kinds, as well as the rules and models for outlooks, attitudes, and behaviors appropriate for each setting.

Using this cultural perspective as a springboard, here is a general overview of each of the seven wisdom books of the Bible. Each overview will present the following pieces of information:

A. The author.

B. A general outline of the book.

C. Wherever appropriate, cultural perspective notes drawn from studies of Mediterranean culture that shed fresh light on these ancient books will be highlighted. Remember to use the five tools mentioned above to discover other cultural perspectives on your own.

I. PROVERBS

A. Who wrote Proverbs?

Proverbs 1:1 leads a reader to believe that Solomon, King David's son, is the author of this collection of sayings.

An old tradition (see 1 Kings 4:29–34) about Solomon prompted many to attribute all wise sayings to him, but it is clear that some of the wise sayings collected here reach back as far as 3000 B.C. and the Sumerian civilization, while others surely derive from a time after Solomon died.

Cultural perspective
Proverbs, brief verses, riddles, ballads, "one-liners," are important *mirrors of the attitudes* of large groups like a tribe, a society or even a nation. Folk wisdom is the result of the creative contribution of many generations of people to their culture, a total way of life. For this reason, proverbs are capable of *illustrating many themes of a culture*. All proverbs deal in some way with *mastering life*, learning the attitudes and behaviors that are appropriate and inappropriate for a wide variety of human experiences. In this part of the program, Proverbs will be a major focus of attention, serving as one large and revealing window for looking into Mediterranean culture.

B. How is the book divided?

The book has seven sections, each with its own "label":

1. Chapters 1–9. "The Proverbs of Solomon, Son of David"

2. Chapters 10–22. "Proverbs of Solomon"

3. Chapters 22:17—24:22. "The Sayings of the Wise"

4. Chapter 24:23–34. "Also the Sayings of the Wise"

5. Chapters 25–29. "More Proverbs of Solomon, Copied by the Men of Hezekiah, King of Judah"

6. Chapter 30. "The Sayings of Agur, Son of Jakeh: An Oracle"

7. Chapter 31. "The Sayings of King Lemuel: An Oracle"

Proverbs 1–9 is a carefully shaped introduction to the rest of the book and describes wisdom as a way of life, or pattern of living. A discerning reader will note how some of the advice given in these chapters is peculiar to the Mediterranean world. Be sure to jot these peculiarities down.

This prologue was probably added to the other collections at the very last stage of development of this interesting book. The other six sections are chiefly collections of individual proverbs with no apparent reason governing the arrangement or ordering of the sayings.

In this book of the program, Proverbs (and Sirach) will be a major resource. The reader who would like to study Proverbs in greater depth is advised to consult one of the following excellent treatments:

Boadt, Lawrence, C.S.P. "Proverbs," in *The Collegeville Bible Commentary*, pp. 644–674.

Fontaine, Carole R. "Proverbs," in *Harper's Bible Commentary*, pp. 495–517.

II. Sirach (Ecclesiasticus)

A. *Who wrote Sirach (Ecclesiasticus)?*

See Sirach 50:25–29 for a rare example of a biblical author's self-identification. How does the author identify himself there? What name is given? How, then, did this book get its Hebrew title?

The original Hebrew text was lost until the years 1896-1900, when a partial copy was found in Cairo. Some other fragments were found in Qumran in 1947, and another partial copy was found at Masada in 1964.

The foreword to the Greek translation (around 132 or 117 B.C.) of this Hebrew original (190 to 175 B.C.) by the author's grandson offers additional information about the author and the times in which he lived.

Cultural perspective

It is virtually impossible for us to ever learn more concrete details about this author. But a consideration of the topics he discusses, the advice he offers, and other details can help us make an intelligent guess regarding the author's age, gender, and social status. (These are the *social variables* a Bible reader might strive to uncover in the text. What clues to these variables can you find? Is the author young or old? Is the author a man or woman? Is the author of high or low social status?

B. How is the book divided?

The book is not easily divided into an outline that makes sense to a modern, western reader. Like chapters 44–50 which the author entitled "In Praise of Famous Men," and which treat a unified theme, the rest of the book tends to cluster many sayings on the same topic close together. In between there are reflections, hymns, proverbs, poems, and essays. Some of these will be presented in subsequent sessions.

Cultural perspective

Sirach lived and wrote in the aftermath of Alexander the Great's conquest of the world in 332 B.C. and during the continuing and growing pressure for all the world to adopt Greek culture. Many Jews felt that the traditions of their ancestors were inadequate for coping with the demands of rapidly changing social and political structures. To comfort and strengthen his compatriots, Sirach affirmed that true wisdom was to be found essentially in Jerusalem rather than Athens. He extols law and fear of the Lord as true wisdom.

At the same time, Sirach incorporated many non-Jewish (that is, Greek and Egyptian) ideas into his writing when he found they could be integrated with his faith.

READ Sirach 30:14–20 and 38:1–15 and observe how he struggles to integrate Jewish and Greek cultural ideas about health, sickness, and healers.

Which are the Jewish ideas?

Which ones are the new Greek ideas?

READ the cluster of comments Sirach offers on wealth in:

10:29–30

11:10–11, 14, 18–19, 23–28

13:17—14:10

25:2–3

26:19–27—27:3

31:1–11

Can you draw any generalizations about wealth from these passages? Was the author wealthy?

In the Palestine of Sirach's day, about ninety percent of the population were peasants and ten percent or even less were the elite. In Jerusalem, where Sirach lived, as in all pre-industrial cities, only ten percent of the population controlled by that city actually resided inside the city limits. The remainder lived in villages or the countryside outside the city walls. Of the urban population—those who lived within the walls—only one or two percent of the population was elite.

Sirach's reflections and concerns about wealth, therefore, probably reflect upper-class life and upper-class culture. The *pattern of life* peculiar to that part of the population is just one of *many possible patterns of life* that constitute the sum total of a way of life which we call culture.

Even so, Sirach recognizes that human life is shot through with ambiguity and uncertainty, and that there are limits to human knowledge. This is why wisdom, for Sirach, amounts to guidelines for human action, answers for the challenging situations that arise in ordinary daily human life.

In this program, we will also focus on Sirach as another window into the Mediterranean culture of our ancestors in the faith. Those who want to study Sirach in still greater detail may consult:

Crenshaw, James L. "Sirach," *Harper's Bible Commentary,* pp. 836–854.
Rybolt, John E., C.M. "Sirach," in *The Collegeville Bible Commentary,* pp. 722–753.
Skehan, Patrick A. and Alexander A. Di Lella. *The Wisdom of Ben Sira.* Anchor Bible, 39.

III. QOHELETH (ECCLESIASTES)

A. Who wrote Qoheleth (Ecclesiastes)?

Even though Ecclesiastes 1:1 proposes that "David's son, Qoheleth, king in Jerusalem" wrote this book, all the internal evidence (Hebrew style, and content) reflects a period of time long after David's son-king (Solomon) died. We simply do not know the exact identity of this author. The words Qoheleth (Hebrew) and Ecclesiastes (Greek) are not names like Harry or Paul, but rather descriptions of a function: "preacher" or "leader of the assembly." Scholars agree that this author is undoubtedly a sage, a wise teacher who is writing his observations after a lifetime of experience and reflection.

As you read this book, what clues can you find in the text that support the scholars' conclusions about the author's identity relative to social standing?

B. How is the book divided?

Introduction: 1:1–11

Part One: Qoheleth's Investigation of Life: Its Purpose, Meaning and Values, 1:12–6:9

Part Two: Qoheleth's Conclusions Drawn from That Investigation, 6:10–12:8

Epilogue: 12:9–14

Cultural perspective

Some modern western readers consider this book to be the most pessimistic in the Bible. Within his cultural context, however, it is perhaps more correct to say that Qoheleth has doubts about traditional answers to life's problems, but isn't yet convinced that the new answers offered by rational Greek thought are an improvement. Like Sirach, Qoheleth offers a window on the *clash between two cultures:* Jewish and Greek. The reader may want to keep a keen eye out for these attitudes as they may be reflected in other wisdom literature: the traditional and conservative in contrast to openness to new positions.

READ Qoheleth 1:12–6:9.

What does he think about pleasure in life (2:1–12)?

What is Qoheleth's opinion about learning, education (2:13–17)?

What are his reflections upon work (2:18–6:9)?

What do you think about the refrain Qoheleth repeats throughout his reflection: Eat, drink, enjoy life with your spouse, etc.?

Cultural setting
The author's adoption of "Solomon" as his pseudonym (1:12), his political-life parables (2:4–10; 4:13–16; 9:14–15), and his exhortation to obey kings, suggest that Qoheleth was a sage in government service. The editor who wrote Qoheleth's epilogue (12:8–13) indicates he also "taught the people knowledge." Would this mean he was a "moonlighter" or felt obliged to teach his people out of a sense of duty or patriotism? How can you tell?

READ 5:7–8.

What should not shock an observer?

Who is watching whom?

What kind of people would want a king who favors agriculture?

These verses seem to make best sense in the cultural context of the years 323 B.C. when the Ptolemies (Greeks in Egypt) administered Palestine. The Ptolemies allowed layers of administration ("the high official has another higher than he watching him") which stimulated rivalry and corruption ("oppression of the poor, and violation of rights and justice in the realm"). The fruits of agriculture were aimed at export rather than the benefit of the native population. Hence the production of wine and oil (export items) dominated over the production of grain and vegetables (subsistence staples). Qoheleth yearns for a "pro-agriculture" king who would care for the people rather than for the elite and the royal coffers.

> READ 8:2–9. Is Qoheleth's advice against criticizing the king a strategy dictated by concern for or worry over his own government position?
>
> In the overall message of this book, would you agree that Qoheleth feels that both God and government are too removed from the people?
>
> Would it be fair to say Qoheleth's sane conclusion in his powerless situation is to work well, enjoy his family, worship dutifully, and share with those who will listen to his advice that life is not nearly as meaningful or moral as traditional wisdom (Proverbs; Sirach) tells us?

We will not return to Qoheleth again during this program. If his work still interests you, you may want to pursue some of the presentations below and study them at your leisure:

Crenshaw, James L. "Ecclesiastes," *Harper's Bible Commentary,* pp. 518–524.

Fischer, James, C.M., "Ecclesiastes," *The Collegeville Bible Commentary,* pp. 812–821.

IV. THE WISDOM OF SOLOMON

A. *Who wrote the book of Wisdom?*

Once again an anonymous author hides behind the name of Solomon. From the work itself, the author stands out clearly as a pious, well-educated Jew who, though familiar with Greek philosophy and Greek culture, remained essentially loyal to the law of God. Yet even while supporting traditional belief, he was open to cultural adaptation.

Cultural adaptation:

> READ 1:16–2:24.

Pagans (or Jewish apostates) are presented as seeing no hope beyond this life. After death, the human spirit "will be poured abroad like unresisting air" (2:3).

The author replies by noting: "God formed the human person for incorruption" (2:23–24) borrowing a Greek term (*incorruption*) from Epicurean philosophy but giving it new meaning. The Greek philosophers believed incorruption to be a divine quality that kept the gods "intact." By assigning this characteristic to human beings, the author of Wisdom raises human immortality to the divine sphere, and further implies that immortality is a pure divine gift to human beings.

Cultural setting

The Greek language of the book of Wisdom reflects the upper-class language of Alexandria in Egypt, which was the largest center of Jewish life in that country. As just noted above, the author is thoroughly familiar with Greek life-style, art, literature, and philosophy. The tension between Judaism and the very appealing Hellenistic philosophy in all its forms is the cultural setting of the book of Wisdom. The author wants to prove beyond doubt to his co-religionists that Israel's revelation is far superior to anything these competing philosophies might offer.

B. How is the book divided?

There are three main divisions to this book:

Part One: A Powerful Exhortation to Blessed Immortality (1:1—6:21)

Part Two: Solomon Praises Lady Wisdom, God's Throne Partner (6:22—11:1)

Part Three: Praise of God as Israel's True Liberator (11:2—19:22).

Cultural perspective
The author had to address some key ideas of Hellenistic culture that were very popular and appealing: immortality; the Isis cult; and ideal kings.

1. Immortality. Epicurean philosophers speculated about *immortality,* making it an integral question for anyone who was concerned with the *meaning and purpose of life.* See the comment above under "Who wrote the book of Wisdom?" to recall how the author countered the Epicurean notions.

2. The Isis cult. A popular religion in Hellenized Egypt devoted to the goddess Isis, this cult exerted a powerful attraction to all—including devout Jews—who became familiar with it.

The goddess Isis had deep roots in ancient Egyptian culture. She was worshiped widely in the Mediterranean world as patroness of culture and great benefactor of humanity. Isis was the best-loved of all the goddesses in the Mediterranean world because of her warm humanity and because she symbolized all the best aspects of woman as lover, wife, mother, and widow. She is a symbol of all things feminine. Special litanies called *aretalogies* praised her outstanding accomplishments in promoting human culture.

Isis is a goddess of the "Mystery Religions." These deities have suffered pain, loss, or death, just like human beings, and this experience gives them a sense of compassion for human sufferings and joys. Isis' consort/brother, Osiris, was slain and resurrected. It should be apparent that Isis would be a very appealing goddess because of her human-like experiences.

Lady Wisdom:

READ Wisdom 6:12-21, where the author presents God's consort as Lady Wisdom, "resplendent and unfading," deliberately drawing a parallel with Isis. All readers familiar with Isis would recognize the parallel. The author argues that the "immortality" or "incorruptibility" which Jews might be tempted to see in Isis can be found in Lady Wisdom (see 6:18-19).

READ Wisdom 7:22—8:16 to appreciate the author's description of Lady Wisdom and her gifts, and then 10:1-21 to learn how she has aided Israel's heroes.

How important is an understanding of the Isis cult to a proper understanding of the book of Wisdom? Would it be possible to draw any conclusions or lessons from Wisdom without appreciating what the author was "really" up to? Where would you go to learn more about Isis? Do Isis and Lady Wisdom remind you of any other famous women? Who are they?

3. Ideal kings. After the death of Alexander the Great (around 332 B.C.), the generals who succeeded him called upon philosophers to train the children of leaders in the virtues needed to be good rulers. These leaders wanted subsequent generations of leaders to imitate Alexander as a benefactor of humanity. In time the philosophers composed books called "kingship tracts" which served as self-help manuals to assist leaders in developing these necessary virtues.

READ Wisdom 6:21–25 and notice that the author advises leaders and rulers to heed Lady Wisdom rather than read the "kingship tracts." This will turn the Jewish intellectuals, for whom this book was written, into "kings," that is, loyal worshipers of the Lord who will uphold his law and superior religious tradition in this searching world. What the world needs is the revelation of Judaism and not "kingship tracts."

READ Wisdom 7:1–22 where "Solomon" (the alleged author) describes how he became a good king.

We will not return to the book of Wisdom again in this program, but those who are interested in pursuing this study further might consult one of the following highly recommended sources:

Boadt, Lawrence, C.S.P. *Reading the Old Testament,* pp. 488–489.

Reese, James M. "Wisdom of Solomon," in *Harper's Bible Commentary,* pp. 820–835.

Rybolt, John E. "Wisdom," in *The Collegeville Bible Commentary,* pp. 701–721.

V. JOB

A. Who wrote the book of Job?

Certainly *not* a man named Job. Actually, the author of
this book is unknown, and the time frame in which it was
written is not known for certain. Very likely the book was
written sometime around 500 B.C., that is, before, during,
or after the exile of the Jews in Babylon (587–537 B.C.).

B. How is the book divided?

A reading of this book indicates that it seems to combine
two different stories of Job's experience. The Prologue
(1:1–2:13) and the Epilogue (42:7–17) say nothing con-
demnatory about Job. It is a simple story of a wise man
whom God tested and found faithful. Whatever was lost
in the test was restored in the reward for fidelity.

The longer story (with some additions) is contained in
chapters 3 through 41 and consists principally of cycles of
speeches between Job and three friends. While Job insists
on his innocence, his friends tell him to confess his guilt.
Only then can God forgive him and restore his fortune.

A simple outline of Job is:

I. The Prologue (1:1–2:13). The just Job loses everything and three friends come to console him.

II. Poetic Dialogue (3:1–31:40). Job laments in bit-
terness, the three friends argue in defense of God.
Job ends with an oath of innocence.

III. Elihu Speeches (32:1–37:24). Little that is new or
helpful is offered by a youth.

IV. Yahweh Speeches (38:1–42:6). God overwhelms
Job and reduces him to silence.

V. The Epilogue (42:7–17). Job is restored.

Cultural perspectives

1. Tribal Culture. Job is a tribal patriarch and as such has to be concerned about the permanence and endurance of his tribe. Land, possessions, descendants, prosperity are major concerns. Job had no hazard insurance to reimburse his losses; there were no federal funds to meet his emergency. Job's confusion arises because he has done everything that should have guaranteed his good fortune, but it didn't.

Another characteristic of tribal culture is oral communication. Take extra care to notice not only *what* is said in the book, but *how* it is said. For instance, in one of his direct appeals to God, Job makes a Hebrew pun on his own name saying the equivalent of, "Do you, Lord, make Job (*'iyyob*) your enemy (*'oyeb*)?" (see 13:24). Granted, the reader is not expected to know Hebrew, but much is hidden in the text even in English translation that a culturally sensitive person could discover.

For instance, Job makes bold to take his case directly to God saying, "I will take my flesh in my teeth" (13:14). Where does this imagery come from? What does a contemporary of Job imagine when this sentence is spoken? How do *you* determine what it means? This is certainly a challenge for the reader to seek out the *connotations* of the words used.

2. Honor and shame. In session three of this program, we will focus in detail on the pivotal values of Mediterranean culture: honor and shame. Honor is a public claim to worth *and* a public acknowledgment or recognition of that worth by others. Shame is the loss of honor. What would Job's material losses (family members, goods, etc.) indicate about his honorable standing in this society? Would his insistence on being a just and innocent person be convincing? In the end, only God can restore his honor by restoring Job to his previous social status in his community.

3. Suffering and pain. In session four of this program, we will examine in some detail physical discipline and the value of physical suffering in the Bible.

> READ Job 2:7 and reflect on the kind of culture that would imagine a God "testing" a faithful believer with physical ailments ("severe boils" from head to toe, 2:7).

> Since everything we know and say about God is based on human experience, what kind of human experience would stimulate the formation of an idea of a God who physically punishes his creatures?

> What kind of culture would admire a person who "grins and bears it?"

> What kind of culture values a man who can bear physical pain without flinching?

> Would such cultural convictions color the way one might imagine God to be like?

4. Friendship. In session five of this program, we will consider a characteristic form of relationship in the Mediterranean known as *dyadic personality*—other-centered relationships. A dyadic personality depends very strongly on the opinions of others for personal self-knowledge, self-assessment, self-worth. This is certainly involved in the role of "friend."

Job's friends behave just as the culture expects. But when Job refuses to heed his friends, how would anyone in his culture judge him? Would anyone believe Job instead of his friends? What does Job mean when he says "only the jackal is my friend" (30:29)?

C. Conclusion

Job is a challenge to complacent orthodoxy. Still, Job cannot be dogmatic about his righteousness and believe he can explain everything. The book may be saying that only God, the all-wise, is entitled to be a dogmatist. That God, in fact, is not a dogmatist can be plainly seen by looking at the irony, ludicrousness, and absurdity of what God has created. Behind the sharp satire of Yahweh's speech, there seems to lurk the idea that God does not have evil and suffering totally under control and, consequently, it would seem that God also suffers.

The pedestrian ending of the folk tale (life must go on) makes even of the tormented book of Job not a tragedy but a comedy, since the central figure is brought back into community with other humans and with God after extreme isolation and alienation.

Probably the author is satisfied if his "whistle blowing" on moralism and dogmatism manage to alert the custodians of wisdom to the perils of cheapening and betraying its critical powers of observation and reflection.

For further study of Job consult:

Boadt, Lawrence, C.S.P. *Reading the Old Testament,* pp. 481–483.
Good, Edwin M., "Job," in *Harper's Bible Commentary,* pp. 407–432.
Gutierrez, Gustavo. *On Job: God-Talk and the Suffering of the Innocent.* Maryknoll, 1987.
Vawter, Bruce. *Job and Jonah: Questioning the Hidden God.* Paulist, 1983.

VI. (WISDOM) PSALMS

A. Who wrote the Psalms?

About half the psalms are attributed to King David, one each is attributed to Moses, Solomon, Heman and Ethan. Other psalms are linked with groups of temple singers, such as "the sons of Korah" and "the sons of Asaph." About one-third have no name attached to them. In truth, these "labels" do not identify the authors but rather designate a collection under that given name. The person identified could have collected some, written some, or simply gathered some psalms that related to the office held by that person.

B. How is the book of Psalms divided?

The one hundred and fifty psalms in the Bible are not gathered in any noticeable order of themes or subjects, but the entire collection is presented in five sections or "books":

Book 1—Psalms 1–41: an early collection of Davidic hymns;

Book 2—Psalms 42–72: a northern collection of hymns;

Book 3—Psalms 73–89: a collection from the temple singers;

Book 4—Psalms 90–106: psalms from a royal collection;

Book 5—Psalms 107–150: a second and expanded Davidic royal collection.

At the end of each "book" there is a special prayer and blessing of praises to serve as the last phrase and mark the conclusion of that "book": "Blessed be the Lord the God of Israel for all eternity and forever. Amen, amen" (see 41:14).

C. Other Categories

The one hundred and fifty psalms can also be clustered by "type" into six general types:

1. Hymns of praise, e.g., Psalm 8;

2. Thanksgiving hymns, e.g., Psalm 18;

3. Individual laments, e.g., Psalm 22;

4. Community laments, e.g., Psalm 12;

5. Royal psalms honoring either God as king or a human king who serves in God's place, e.g., Psalm 2;

6. Wisdom Psalms: 1; 19; 25; 32; 34; 36; 37; 49; 62; 73; 75; 78; 111; 112; 119; 127; 128.

A psalm of individual lament will be subsequently examined in detail to illustrate a specific dimension of Mediterranean culture. For the present, let us focus attention on the Wisdom psalms.

D. Wisdom Psalms

These psalms reflect the piety of sophisticated scribes, and they generally take as their theme, like other wisdom literature, the notion of retribution for sin and evil and reward for goodness. This belief contrasts with contradictory human experience wherein good people suffer and evil people prosper.

Some common features of these psalms are:

1. Key words like "wisdom," "fear of the Lord," the direct address "sons";

2. Stylistic devices like beatitudes ("happy the person who...."), question-and-answer verses;

3. Emphasis on teaching and warning;

4. Themes of unjust suffering, the evil rich people, God's special protection and guidance of the pious ones, and contrasts between the way of obedience that leads to life and disobedience that leads to death.

Cultural relevance

Every culture socializes its members into knowing the "correct way things should be" and the "incorrect or improper way that things sometimes are." People are recognized as successful and feel satisfaction when things are the way they ought to be. When things go awry, people are disoriented. Thus, the one hundred and fifty psalms can be clustered into a different, three-part group:

I. Psalms of orientation

These psalms reflect the seasons of well-being in human life. They are characterized by sentiments of gratitude for God's fidelity. God is reliable, his creation is constant, his laws are reliable. Culture works! God's in his heaven, and all's right with the world.

READ Psalms 1, 8, 112.

II. Psalms of disorientation

These psalms suit the anguished seasons of life's hurts, periods of alienation, suffering, and death. The culturally well-ordered world of the psalmist has fallen apart. The sentiments these psalms reflect are rage, resentment, self-pity, hatred, shame, isolation, despair, hostility. Culture has lost its meaning. Things are not as they ought to be.

READ Psalms 35, 74, 88.

III. Psalms of reorientation

These psalms reflect a life situation set right-side-up once more. The human being has experienced turns of surprise along the downward path. A new gift of God overwhelms the previous despair and inspires joy. Sentiments reflected here are delight, awe, gratitude, wonder, thanksgiving. Fortunes have been reversed, rescue is experienced, deliverance is most welcome. Culture really does work, though perhaps not as simply as was previously believed.

READ Psalms 30 (an individual voice); 124 (a group).

Psychology versus society. Americans are a very introspective people. Their first inclination in reading the psalms from the threefold perspective just suggested is to read them in an eminently personal, individualistic way. Such a perspective will seek a *psychological* interpretation. What's going on inside me? Can I relate my feelings to these feelings? What does the text say to me?

American readers need to be challenged to take up a *societal* interpretation. What is going on in society or the culture that has prompted the psalmist to experience a cultural breakdown, a cultural frustration, cultural disappointment? What social rule is no longer working? What is going on or not going on in the community? In session five we will discover how inescapably "communal" the seemingly "individualistic" sentiments of the Mediterranean psalmist really are.

Stereotypical language. As you read the psalms, make a list of the words that are regularly repeated. For instance, which words seem to prevail in laments? Which words prevail in wisdom psalms? Is the list long? Are the words varied, or do a handful of words seem to be used with regularity? If this seems to be a list of "stereotypical" sentiments, is it possible to conclude that the psalmist perceives self as a stereotype of a "suffering person," "a wise person," etc.? Would it seem that the culture does not permit an expression of "individual uniqueness"?

Socioeconomic conflict. Read some psalms of individual lamentation and notice that powerful people (often the "rich" and the "wicked") seem to oppress people in a lower social position ("the poor" and "the innocent").

Do oppression and fraud appear often in the complaints?

How often are deceitful speech, false testimony, and bribes mentioned in these psalms?

What role do social institutions and certain individuals play in the psalms you have read: e.g., the king, the law, the priests?

What kind of cultural picture does such a reading of the psalms help you to compose?

For further study of the psalms, consult:

Stuhlmueller, Carroll, C.P. *Psalms.* 2 volumes. Wilmington, DE.: Michael Glazier, 1983.

VII. THE SONG OF SONGS

A. Who wrote the Song of Songs?

Though attributed to King Solomon, this collection of love poems gives evidence of having been composed, edited, and expanded over a period that may have extended from 950 B.C. to 200 B.C. Very likely many voices and many hands over many centuries contributed to the development of this collection as we have it today.

B. How is it divided?

Attempts at discerning a structure in this collection of poems have not been successful. The Song of Songs is best considered a collection of about twenty-five independent poems strung together by a story line of boy and girl in love, longing for one another, imagining various opportunities and assuming imaginary roles, yet frustrated in actually meeting one another. The reader is best advised to read and enjoy.

Cultural perspective

The Wasf. Read Song of Songs 4:1–7; 5:9–16; 6:4–7; and 6:13–7:5. These colorful descriptions of the human body are very similar to traditional Arabic wedding songs called *wasfs* which praise the bride's or groom's body. While modern researchers first discovered these songs in the late 19th century in their investigations of Arab village life, the songs have been around for centuries, if not millennia. Until very recently the peasant culture of the Middle East has remained relatively constant and unchanged for thousands of years.

Though the Song of Songs is the only place in the Bible where *wasfs* are found, they are very common throughout Middle-Eastern cultures. The *wasf* describes the human body in sequence: top to bottom, or bottom to top, with metaphors drawn from nature and from architecture. The metaphors appeal to sight (hair like a flock of goats that winds down Mount Gilead) as well as to other senses like touch (breasts like fawns) or smell and taste (lips like lilies, distilling liquid myrrh).

Contexts. The poems take place in one or a combination of four different contexts. Find the poems or sections that are set in the following contexts. Take note of the effect of the context or setting on the behavior of the lovers:

1. The habitable countryside
2. Wild or remote nature
3. Interior space (homes, halls, bedrooms)
4. City streets.

Themes. Read the poems once again and single out various themes such as togetherness, separation, the power and beauty of love, eating and drinking, that serve as erotic metaphors.

Relationships. Note well what the boy and girl each do separately, and what they do or do not do together. In session three of this program, we will learn more about honorable and shameful behavior for men and women, and in session four (parenting), we will discover the strict segregation of sexes required after puberty in this culture. In what ways do the behavior of boy and girl in the poems of the Song of Songs run contrary to the wisdom offered by Proverbs and Sirach? Could the behavior described in the Song of Songs be possible? For whom and under what circumstances?

Cultural Note:

> In the light of what you have read about the proper behavior of men and women in Proverbs, Sirach, and elsewhere in the Bible, where and when would the behavior described in the Song of Songs take place?

> When would a boy or girl be permitted to be together or meet together, just the two of them? If such a meeting is permitted, why is it not reported more often in the Bible? If such a meeting is not permitted, what is likely to happen if they get caught? Would any boy or girl in the culture risk getting caught in such behavior?

These poems need to be situated and understood in the context of the total Mediterranean culture:

1. Because the Song of Songs. like the *wasf,* is a wedding song, it is sung in a "safe" place: the well-guarded and carefully regulated company of the extended family. No one would have an opportunity to misbehave, since everyone in this enormously extended family keeps an eye on everyone else.

2. In this very same extended family context, the newly-married couple are now "given permission" to put their previous fantasies (the sentiments of the song) into action (the duties of marriage) at the right time and in the right place. This wedding song forms part of the "warm up" for the occasion.

3. In the Mediterranean world of antiquity, as well as the present, the universal cultural belief is that any time a boy and girl or man and woman are alone, unchaperoned, for even the briefest moment, they will certainly yield to lust and have sexual relations. For this reason, women always travel in groups and/or with children; men, too, congregate alone.

4. The Mediterranean world does not distinguish sharply between appearance and reality. Often appearance substitutes for reality. The boy who told his father he'd go to work in the field but then changed his mind and didn't go, simply allowed the appearance (promise) to substitute for the reality (actual work). Similarly, the most culturally plausible interpretation of the Song of Songs is that the imagined erotic scenes between two unmarried people in the Song of Songs (appearance) are a mental substitute for a strictly forbidden reality.

We will not return again to the Song of Songs, but those interested in studying it in greater depth are encouraged to consult:

Falk, Marcia. "Song of Songs," in *Harper's Bible Commentary,* pp. 525–528.

Murphy, Roland E. "Canticles," in *Wisdom Literature: Job, Proverbs, Ruth, Canticles, Ecclesiastes, and Esther.* Grand Rapids, Eerdmans, pp. 97–124.

Tournay, Raymond Jacques, O.P. *Word of God, Song of Love: A Commentary on the Song of Songs.* New York/Mahwah: Paulist.

Trible, Phyllis. "Love's Lyrics Redeemed," in *God and the Rhetoric of Sexuality,* Philadelphia: Fortress, pp. 144–165.

CONCLUSION

The observant reader who has carefully examined these books of wisdom cannot help but notice that, overall, the books present two opposing viewpoints: "traditional wisdom" as exemplified in Proverbs and Sirach and "viewpoints or reflections that challenge this complacent tradition" as illustrated in Job or Wisdom. The careful reading and study of this portion of the Bible will reward the learner with insights into the Mediterranean culture in which all biblical literature originated. A knowledge of this culture is absolutely essential to understanding who is supporting it; who is challenging it; and how very much of it has continued unchanged over thousands of years.

FOLLOW-UP

Some readers may want to spend more time examining in greater detail one or another of the wisdom books reviewed just above. In so doing, they will have added opportunity to develop a sensitivity to the Mediterranean culture reflected in these books. It is strongly recommended that the reader who chooses to study one of the wisdom books at this point remember to take along the "culture-sensitizing tools" identified at the beginning of this session:

1. Be curious about everything!
2. Notice culturally-conditioned behavior in the text.
3. Observe cultural connotations of words, especially when the meaning is not immediately clear.
4. Search for clues to social variables (age, gender, social class) in the texts.
5. Take note of conventional behavior in common human situations.

The information unearthed from the text by the use of these tools will very likely not be routinely found in the books listed as "recommended readings" in this program. In this regard, the present reader will be a discoverer, a pioneer.

Other readers may be convinced that a good follow-up to this lesson is to move ahead to the next lesson. This is also a good decision. Don't forget to bring along the tools!

Session Three

Core Cultural Values

E very culture has a central cluster of values that control all aspects of life in that culture. A value is a broad principle or guide to behavior which is transmitted from generation to generation, often for thousands of years without change and which directs the daily life of all of society's members. Values provide patterns for living, criteria for making decisions, and yardsticks by which to evaluate oneself and others. This central cluster of values comprises the "core" values of a society.

Generally speaking, the core values of Mediterranean culture are "honor and shame." The corresponding value in American society is "guilt"; honor and shame do not play key roles in American culture.

Preparation: View the film *Prizzi's Honor.* Become acquainted with the notions of guilt, shame, and honor.

Lesson: Read selections from Ben Sirach and Proverbs with a view to identifying Mediterranean core cultural values of "honor and shame."

Follow-up: View the film *Prizzi's Honor* a second time.

PREPARATION

If possible, view the film *Prizzi's Honor,* or read the book upon which it was based: Richard Condon, *Prizzi's Honor.* If it is not possible to do this, the reader may skip to the next section which explains the notion of core values. Even so, a cursory reading of what follows may prove enlightening and useful.

The story of *Prizzi's Honor* involves characters from two families: the Prizzi family and the Partanna family. In the Prizzi family, the chief characters are: the father, Don Corrado Prizzi; his sons, including Dominic and Eduardo; and Mae Rose Prizzi, Dominic's daughter. Don Corrado Prizzi is a friend of Angelo Partanna and the godfather of his son, Charlie Partanna.

The story line revolves around the relationship of Charlie Partanna, the adult, to many members of the Prizzi family, but especially to Don Corrado Prizzi, Dominic Prizzi, and Dominic's daughter, Mae Rose Prizzi.

Charlie's relationship with an outsider to both families, Irene Walker (Walcewicz), is a key to understanding the film's (and book's) title: *Prizzi's Honor.* Charlie marries Irene, much to Mae Rose Prizzi's disappointment.

As you view the film or read the book, pay attention to the many uses of the word "honor" and "shame" (or "dishonor"). Notice the context in which these words appear; they are closely associated with the understanding of "family."

In particular, pay very careful attention to scenes close to the end of the movie. The scene that viewers may want to watch more than once and study closely is that in which Don Corrado and other family members persuade Charlie of what he must do to make up "for the great sin *against your honor* for covering up [your wife's part] in the Vegas scam."

Charlie knows that his wife, Irene, has wronged the Prizzi family in Las Vegas. She stole $720,000. When Don

Corrado and other family members discover her role, they urge Charlie to take a drastic measure: kill his wife. When Charlie balks, they tell him: "What is pain, compared to the *honor* of the Prizzi's?" Moreover, they add, "It would be different if she was one of us, but she was never really part of the family." As Charlie continues to resist with every reason he can think of, they are relentless in their resolve: "She is your wife, but *we are your life!*" and "*We are your blood!*"

After viewing this film and discussing especially the concluding scenes, consider these reflections on "core cultural values."

CORE CULTURAL VALUES

Core cultural values guide and control all aspects of life in a given culture. These values differ from culture to culture, and indeed those of mainstream United States culture are significantly different from the core values of the Mediterranean world.

Mainstream United States

Experts tell us that the core or central value of mainstream United States culture is "instrumental activism." This is very clear from our emphasis on activity, on doing, on achieving, on setting goals and priorities and then pursuing them with determination until they are achieved. The "rules" for doing, achieving, setting goals, and the like are known by everybody in this culture. They are taught to each person from early childhood, and they become internalized monitors of human behavior. These values are reflected and reinforced in the sports of each society. The trinity of sports invented or developed in America (baseball, basketball, football) reflect the core values of equality, competition, fair play, all geared to obtaining the goal: winning the game.

Each of us is concerned or anxious about doing, achieving, competing, reaching goals, winning, and the like. We routinely worry about such things. When we think or know that we have succeeded, we feel good, satisfied, warm all over. When we think or know we have failed, we feel bad, dissatisfied, and guilty. Experts point out that such anxiety and guilt characterize all cultures, but in mainstream U.S. culture these feelings force citizens to behave in a certain way. In other words, anxiety and guilt are powerfully motivating values in mainstream U.S. culture. This is true of any inner-directed society whose members are expected to have strongly individualized and internalized controls over behavior.

The Mediterranean World

The central or core value of our Mediterranean ancestors in the faith is "interpersonal contentment." This value dictates that people should be content with what they have and not worry about getting ahead of others, achieving more than others, or being better than others. This, in fact, is what Mediterranean people are "anxious" about: not to infringe on others, and not to allow others to infringe on them.

Such anxiety revolves especially around the value feeling of "honor" and "shame." Whatever the status into which a person is born is "honorable" and must be maintained throughout life. Indeed, being born into honor is the chief way of getting it. The reason for genealogies in the Bible is to let the reader know that the person to whom this genealogy is applied is honorable because the entire ancestral line is full of honorable people. This is the point of the genealogies in 1 Chronicles 1–10 as well as in Matthew 1 and Luke 3, and elsewhere in the Bible.

Usually in genealogies only the first three and the last three count. The first three on the list are generally known to all people of the culture from its past, and the last three are also known because they can very easily be traced. Contemporaries will personally know the last three and should be able to recognize from "history" the first three. Those in between are thrown in to pad and expand the list.

The honor into which one is born is called *"ascribed" honor*. It is rather passive; the person has done nothing to obtain it. As a matter of fact, the honor really resides in the family of which the individual is a member. This is the reason why the family figures so prominently in the discussion of honor. Genealogies relate "ascribed" honor.

There is an honor other than "ascribed" which can be earned or achieved. It is called *"acquired" honor* and most often is acquired through a social game that goes on in the culture all the time, called "challenge and response." While people are supposed to be "interpersonally content," as a matter of fact they strive to lower another's honor rating and gain a higher one for themselves. This constant challenge to the honor of others goes on particularly between non-family members all the time.

Thus, honor can be defined as a person's or group's claim to worth accompanied by the public, social, acknowledgment of that worth. The common conclusion to many of Jesus' mighty deeds: "And they spread his fame through all the district," or words to that effect, is a description of "acquired" honor.

Shame is the correlative of honor and can be understood in two ways. From a positive view, "shame" is a sensitivity to one's honor and honor rating. Another way of stating this is that an honorable person always has a "sense of shame." Conversely, people who behave dishonorably are called "shameless," or are described as "having no shame."

Shame in a negative sense is what results when an honorable person is dishonored or fails to guard or maintain personal honor. When a person or group loses its honor, or is shamed, the consequences are very serious. In the Mediterranean world, women are considered the repository of honor. Men (fathers, brothers, husbands) are expected to guard their women, watch over their behavior, for it is chiefly through them that honor is lost and the family is shamed. In the film, *Prizzi's Honor*, Dominic Prizzi's daughter, Mae Rose, brought shame to her family by running away and marrying someone other than an approved partner. For this she was disowned and no longer welcome in the family. She was disobedient and therefore disrespectful to her family. When that approved partner, Charlie Partanna, finally married someone else, Mae Rose could be rehabilitated or forgiven and accepted back into the family. The shame the family experienced when Mae Rose jilted her intended partner was removed when Charlie finally did find another partner.

But when Mae Rose tells her father that Charlie, now married to somebody else, forced himself on her sexually, Dominic is livid because Charlie shamed him! Men's honor is challenged through their women. Dominic's only choice is to have Charlie killed. It is the only way that Dominic can remove his shame and regain his honor. If he takes no action and the deed gains publicity, as it surely will in such close-knit family situations, Dominic will become a laughing-stock in the community as a weak man who doesn't know how and is unable to guard the family's honor.

Experts note that anxiety about one's honor and shame exists in all cultures, but in the Mediterranean world it is *the* centrally motivating force behind social control. This would be true of any outer-directed society with strongly socialized sanctions for including and excluding members from that society.

To summarize, this discussion is about how society coerces its members to follow a determined way of life or pattern of behavior. All citizens are anxious about conforming, but inner-directed societies, like the mainstream United States, will feel a sense of guilt for not conforming. Other-directed societies, like our Mediterranean biblical ancestors in the faith, will feel a sense of shame for not conforming.

As we now prepare to begin to read biblical texts, we should be on the lookout for "honor" and "shame" words in these Mediterranean compositions. The biblical texts can be expected to reflect honor and shame concerns as a principal focus. Limiting ourselves to those words alone is a fine place to start, but keeping in mind related words will help the reader realize how much honor and shame values permeate the entire Bible. Here is a list to help readers become tuned in to these central concerns.

Honor: Equivalent words would also include nouns such as glory, blamelessness, repute, fame, and related verbs such as to honor, to glorify, to spread the fame, etc.

Shame: Nouns such as dishonor, disgrace, as well as the related verbs to shame, be ashamed, feel ashamed, to be cheated, and the like.

Dishonor: To scorn, to despise, to revile, to reproach, to rebuke, to insult, to blaspheme, to deride, to mock as well as dishonoring actions such as plucking another's beard, striking the head, spitting upon a person, and so on.

Intention to challenge or to dishonor: Nouns such as test, trap, and verbs such as to tempt and to spy upon. In narratives, all questions should be carefully reviewed to determine whether they are simple inquiries or subtle challenges calling another's honor into question.

Perceptions of being challenged or shamed: Nouns such as vengeance, wrath, anger, and the like.

LESSON: Honor and Shame in Proverbs

How is people's behavior controlled?

Everyone is anxious for approval and usually does what society expects mainly for one of two reasons:

a. external pressure: sensitivity to public opinion, and thus a sense of shame, concern for honor

b. internal pressure: sensitivity to an internalized norm. This is usually described as guilt.

A proverb is a short, poetic saying that either proposes a culturally valuable attitude or behavior, or discourages and forbids a culturally unacceptable attitude or behavior. The biblical book of Proverbs probably took shape in the late sixth century B.C., though many individual sayings reach back to the monarchy (c.1000 B.C.) or even earlier. The proverbs are intended to teach youth how to cope with life in a variety of circumstances and to present as guides for these youth the wisdom gained from experience.

Honor

Consider some of the Proverbs which deal explicitly with "honor." These would include:

Proverbs 3:9

Proverbs 3:16

Proverbs 3:35

Proverbs 4:8

Proverbs 5:9

Proverbs 6:33

Proverbs 8:18

Proverbs 11:16

Proverbs 13:18

Proverbs 14:31

Proverbs 15:33

Proverbs 18:3

Proverbs 18:12

Proverbs 20:3

Proverbs 21:21

Proverbs 22:4

Proverbs 26:1

Proverbs 26:8

Proverbs 27:18

Proverbs 29:23.

For instance, READ Proverbs 13:18

Notice that honor is contrasted with disgrace (and poverty) while instruction and reproof are presented as synonyms. Honor results from heeding instruction, particularly reproof. The book of Proverbs is part of that collection in scripture known as "wisdom literature" which is practical, down-to-earth advice on successful living. Such wisdom helps a person maintain honor. The instruction and reproof mentioned here could refer to parental guidance. (READ Proverbs 1:8–9; 4:1–8.)

In contrast to the rest of the book which contains single and separate sayings, the *first nine chapters of Proverbs* contain fully developed poems. READ the references to honor in these chapters (e.g., 3:9; 3:16; 3:35; 4:8; 5:9; 6:33; 8:18) within the context of the complete poems as indicated in your translations and see whether the "honor" perspective offers a key to understanding.

Remember: The advice presented in Proverbs is intended by the culture to control behavior and attitudes.

Notice the repeated exhortations to "heed" the parent's advice.

READ Proverbs 1:8–9

Proverbs 2:1–5

Proverbs 3:1–2

Proverbs 3:21–22

Proverbs 4:1–9

Proverbs 4:10–13

Proverbs 5:1–2

Proverbs 6:20–23

Proverbs 7:1–5

Proverbs 7:24.

READ these exhortations and make a list of the results of "heeding" wisdom. This will be a list of synonyms for "honor." Honor will include all of these things and more.

Notice the very external and visible aspect of these synonyms: garland; pendants; length of days and years of life. Recall that honor is a claim to worth and a public acknowledgment of that worth.

Why do you think so many of these texts link honor with staying away from "foreign women" (loose woman; adventuress; other synonyms)? What role does a woman play in the concept of honor? What kind of "control" should honor exert on a woman's attitudes and behavior?

SEE 7:10ff: The harlot or loose woman does not stay at home (like an honorable woman should) but (rather) wanders the street and the market-place. Women's behavior is then generalized in the free-standing proverb 11:16: "A gracious woman wins esteem, but she who hates virtue is covered with shame."
   Another set of proverbs link humility with honor:

READ Proverbs 15:33

Proverbs 18:12

Proverbs 22:4

Proverbs 29:23

Proverbs 11:2

Proverbs 16:19

Take note of any other references to "humility" that you can find.

Humility in the biblical world is a value that directs individuals to stay within their inherited status (or their "ascribed" honor). It is shameful to presume on others, or lord it over others, or even appear to do either of these shameful things. Humility is especially pleasing to God: "To the humble [God] shows kindness" (Proverbs 3:34). Jesus cloaks himself with this virtue, too: "I am meek and humble of heart" (Matthew 11:29) and advises those who would follow him to avoid challenging the honor of others (see Matthew 23:12; Luke 14:11; 18:14). Humility is thus a certain claim to neutrality in the normal Mediterranean competition of life. Biblical texts suggest that this posture could be socially acknowledged and respected.

Pause for a moment and discuss whether this virtue, humility, is or can be operative in mainstream U.S. culture. Would it work in the corporate world? How?

Can individual workers be humble and thereby gain great honor?

Would humble workers gain raises and improved benefits or would humble workers be targets of abuse?

Would a humble worker join a labor union? Ask for a raise? Request a longer vacation?

Can humility and its resulting honor work in any United States life context you can imagine?

Shame

In a positive view, shame is a sensitivity to one's honor and a determination to guard and maintain it. In a negative view it is the result of a loss of honor. Here are the proverbs in which shame is mentioned.

READ Proverbs 9:13

Proverbs 10:5

Proverbs 12:4

Proverbs 13:5

Proverbs 14:35

Proverbs 17:2

Proverbs 18:3

Proverbs 19:26

Proverbs 25:8

Proverbs 25:10

Proverbs 28:7

Proverbs 29:15.

Return to Proverbs 1–9, reread the passages mentioning honor and make a list of the words contrasting with honor (e.g., "way of evil," "perverted speech," "crooked paths," "deviousness," "disloyalty," "unfaithfulness or infidelity," etc.). This will provide a list of "shame" words and equip you with an understanding of shame as correlative to honor.

In a positive sense, a person with a sense of shame would strive to avoid these things, as indeed Proverbs strongly urges. In a negative sense, if a person could be characterized by any of these nouns or adjectives, that person would be considered dishonorable or shamed.

Consider Proverbs 12:4. What is a shameful wife compared to?

Healthy bones were considered moist (see 8:3b "drink or refreshment" to the bones); dry bones were not considered healthy, see 17:22; if bones became so dry they rotted, the condition was bad indeed. Now all these phrases are used figuratively at all times. This is after all not a lesson in anatomy, but a comment on a life situation. Dry or rotten bones were a common image for distress and desolation. Thus a wife who brings shame brings great distress and desolation to the husband and the family.

How does a wife bring shame? By not measuring up to the ideal wife as described in 31:10–31. This passage might spark spirited discussion in the group, for the image presented might sound to mainstream U.S. feminine ears like "Supermom." [See the PBS special "The Life and Times of Rosie the Riveter," Program #105 in the *American Experience* series; call PBS Video Services at 1–800–424–7963 for further information.]

Or consider Proverbs 28:7

The topic is "son." An honorable son observes the law, but a son whose pastime is gluttony brings shame to the father. Why so? Gluttony bespeaks having more than enough. The Mediterranean cultural obligation when one has more than enough is to share with those who do not have enough. To be capable of gluttony means one has refused to share, and this is shameful.

Notice who bears the shame. The father is tainted by the son's misbehavior. Honor and shame in the Mediterranean world are never purely personal matters. They are always bound up with groups, especially with the family. The father must bear the shame of an ill-bred son. Recall the pleas of the father in Proverbs 1–9 that the son hear wisdom and keep it.

Much more to the point:

READ Proverbs 19:26.

Recall the commandment: "Honor your father and your mother, that your days may be long in the land which the Lord your God gives you" (Exodus 20:12; Deuteronomy 5:16). Does this commandment shed any light on this passage? If the commandment were being observed, would this proverb be necessary? Would it have survived? Does its survival reveal something about how sons "truly" behaved in spite of commandments?

On another topic, consider Proverbs 25:8,18 and its context, and compare it to Proverbs 20:3.

The Mediterranean world plays a continuous game of challenge and response relative to the honor of non-family members. Practically every question can be considered a challenge that requires a proper response, or else honor can be lost. In this world, taking a neighbor to court is already an admission of defeat, a dishonorable action, because one admits that one is unable to maintain personal honor. The honorable person will strive to negotiate a settlement with the neighbor outside of court, before going to court, in every effort to avoid the court.

The context of 25:8–10 indicates that the witness is going to damage the neighbor in court with factual (true) testimony. In the Mediterranean world this, too, is shameful. In modern, recent times, a maiden betrothed to a cousin let it be known she did not want to marry that cousin, but had in mind another. Even her father did not want to press the marriage he had "arranged." So the male cousin came and kidnapped the maiden to see what kind of resolution he could bargain. The kidnapping was witnessed by the villagers. The aggrieved father of the maiden took the case to court. When summoned to the witness stand, all the witnesses swore they did not know who had kidnapped the maiden! Had these witnesses spoken truthfully what they knew, they would have acted shamefully and dishonorably. As it was, the father had already acted shamefully by taking his grievance to court. When the judge threw the case out of court, the villagers came to the father and agreed to help him resolve his grievance and that of the spurned partner informally among themselves. This is the cultural context of Jesus' reflection in Luke 12:57–59//Matthew 5:25–26.

The word translated as "strife" in 20:3 is often rendered "court case." The honorable man avoids this, but the fool literally "breaks out" in contention at every opportunity. Argumentation is yet another arena of life in which honor and shame must play a restraining role in the Mediterranean world.

Mainstream United States Culture

All human beings are anxious about measuring up to standards, meeting expectations, and achieving goals. In some cultures, external controls are more effective, such as public opinion, widespread publicity, and the like. These cultures are described as "honor" and "shame" cultures. They require their members to *suppress* unacceptable social behavior, as the book of Proverbs has demonstrated. Notice, too, that the basic patterns of life described in these proverbs tend to be situation-centered.

Even a brief reflection on mainstream U.S. culture should indicate that feelings of honor and shame do not exert powerful control over social behavior. In recent memory, a president was forced to resign from office under shameful circumstances, but one would hardly know that from the words spoken and the subsequent behavior of that same individual. A subsequent administration experienced the highest number of indictments in U.S. history of its members in various courts, yet some of these individuals have returned to play another role in the American game known as politics.

The more significant and effective social control of human behavior in mainstream U.S. culture is believed to be a sense of guilt. In this culture, individuals are required to *repress* unacceptable social behavior. Here internal controls are more important than external controls. And the basic patterns of life tend to be individual-centered, which is quite in keeping with mainstream U.S. culture, the most individualistic culture that has ever existed in the history of humankind.

Repression buries painful and unpleasant material deep in the unconscious. The guilt which emerges from such a course of action is often vague and difficult to specify. Repression evokes feelings of guilt. Suppression is dictated by external circumstances, but the thought of such actions is not excluded from consciousness. Suppression evokes feelings of shame.

Here is a chart comparing the three social controls: anxiety, shame, and guilt:

ANXIETY	SHAME	GUILT
loss of calm in a threat	loss of face before persons	loss of integrity in one's conscience
feared vulnerability	fail an ideal or public exposure	condemnation by inner judge
arousal by environment	embarrassment by society	pain by morality
primal emotion fear of loss of being	total emotion fear of social rejection	specific emotion fear of judgment or correction
paralyzing	humiliating	humbling
wants to freeze tries to flee seeks to fight	wants to hide tries to cover denies	wants to justify tries to rationalize excuses
Positive side	**Positive side**	**Positive side**
energizes heightens awareness	stirs discretion energizes honor	gives direction urges integrity
Negative side	**Negative side**	**Negative side**
distracts attention	disrupts social life	destroys inner peace
Solution	**Solution**	**Solution**
anxiety must be released	honor must be regained	guilt needs to be forgiven

Chart based on David Augsberger, *Pastoral Counselling Across Cultures,* p. 122.

As noted before, in every cultural group there are representatives of all three patterns: anxiety, shame, and guilt. The central tendency, however, of any given group can be identified from its values, mores, rules, interpersonal relationships, styles of mediating or negotiating conflict, arts, and literature.

"Guilt" in Biblical Literature

The word "guilt" occurs only rarely in the Bible. The word "shame" occurs about eight times more often than guilt in all of the scriptures. But one needs to be careful about the meaning of the word "guilt" in English-language translations of the Bible. The Hebrew word ordinarily translated "guilt" is *'awon*. Literally it means "crooked" or "distorted" and is used mostly to describe an action against God (see Genesis 4:13). But this Hebrew word is very difficult to define with precision. One thing experts are certain of: Biblical authors do not understand the word "guilt" as an inner feeling of remorse or a bad conscience. They rather perceive it to be a situation that has come about because of a sin committed against God or one's neighbor.

READ Psalm 32, and notice especially verse 5:

I acknowledged my sin (failure; missing the mark) to thee and I did not hide my twisted condition (*'awon*),
I said: "I will confess my transgressions (acts of rebellion) to the Lord";
then you did forgive the crookedness (*'awon*) of my sin (missing the mark).

In some translations, the Hebrew word *'awon* is translated as "guilt" or "iniquity." With this word the biblical authors are describing the consequence, or effect, or result, or damage that derives from sin. In verse 10, the psalmist says: "Many are the pains of the wicked; but steadfast love surrounds him who trusts in the Lord." Pain should be understood here as the result of realizing that one does not enjoy the steadfast love of the Lord. Some would interpret this as mental anguish, but in view of verses 3–4, where the psalmist describes a bodily illness ("my body wasted away," "my strength was dried up") it would be more appropriate to conclude that a bodily illness forced the psalmist to consider himself "guilty" of a transgression against the Lord. The bodily illness produced pain in the realization that he was not experiencing the "steadfast love" of the Lord. This entire condition is what the biblical author calls 'awon. It is the condition resulting from sin, and it is not quite the understanding that mainstream U.S. citizens have of the word "guilt." It would be fair to say, then, that there is slim if any evidence of guilt in the Bible as U.S. mainstream citizens understand guilt. A clearer expression of the same sentiments in explicit honor and shame terms can be read in Psalm 31 immediately preceding this psalm.

Conclusion to the Lesson

In this session, we have focused on core values of a culture as principal means of exercising social control. All persons in every culture develop a sense of anxiety, shame, and guilt, but each culture relies on one of these values more than the other in socializing its citizens. Societies that fear "powers" or "cosmic forces" (demons, spirits, and the like) because they are considered to be in charge of life are guided by *anxiety*. Guilt and shame in these cultures would be largely unconscious. Anxiety, instead, stimulates energies for inhibiting undesirable behavior and directing citizens toward desired goals. This description aptly characterizes tribal societies.

Societies whose social controls are promises of inclusion or threats of exclusion tend to be outer-directed societies, and *shame* is the major force behind behavior. Shame as discretion is shame in a positive sense, and it protects a person from shame as disgrace, or shame in a negative sense, the shame of losing one's honor. Anxiety and guilt do exist but are largely unconscious and may be difficult to identify in written materials. This description is appropriate for Mediterranean societies in general and biblical society in particular.

Societies which depend upon *guilt* for shaping and directing their members' behavior must inculcate internal self-judgment or moral conscience which serves as an "internal parent" laying down rules and judging behavior in each instance. Shame and anxiety are also present, but they are largely repressed and unconscious. This description suits mainstream U.S. culture rather well as social analysts regularly point out.

The vocabulary and concepts in the book of Proverbs reflect honor and shame as principal determinants of social behavior among our ancestors in the faith. Once sensitized to this peculiar (to us) way of thinking, a reader cannot fail to notice it on every page of the Bible.

FOLLOW-UP

1. If possible, a second viewing of the film *Prizzi's Honor* in light of the explanations of honor and shame presented in this chapter will make these features stand out starkly. They will then be clearly seen as powerful forces controlling the behavior of the Mediterranean characters in this film. At the same time, notice which character does not seem to be at all influenced by the force of

honor and shame. Is this character of Mediterranean or different ancestry?

2. The entire book of Proverbs could be read to search for additional perspectives on "honor and shame" as directive values in this culture.

Though the final edition of this biblical book probably emerged in the late sixth century B.C., many sayings in chapters 10–29 undoubtedly originated much earlier, in the monarchy (c.1000 B.C.) or even before. These proverbs were a key means by which parents reared their children and court personnel trained others for service in the royal household.

How then did honor and shame shape behavior in kinship and politics in the biblical world?

3. Consult your favorite guide to understanding the Old Testament and review the outline and background information presented about the book of Proverbs. How has this current session complemented that information?

4. In group discussions of personal experiences of "guilt," "honor," "shame," or other directive values, is there any connection between these experiences and personal ethnic background? At what generational remove from immigration does a person behave more like an American than like the ethnic ancestors?

Resources

Augsburger, David W. *Pastoral Counseling Across Cultures.* Philadelphia: Westminster, 1986. Chapter Four: "Inner Controls, Outer Controls, Balanced Controls," pp. 111–143.

Condon, Richard. *Prizzi's Honor.* Book or videocassette.

Session Four

Parenting (Discipline)

The American value-preference for *guilt* (a private and internal state) as a core value requires a style of parenting and discipline directed toward an individual's *interior* make-up; dialogue and persuasion are paramount so the child will learn self-control.

The Mediterranean value-preference for *shame* (a public and external situation) as a core value requires a style of parenting directed toward an individual's concern for *external* appearances; instilling unquestioning obedience through physical punishment is a preferred strategy. The child must learn to make a good impression on and win the approval of others.

Preparation: Watch a representative TV program focused on a family. Observe the methods of parenting or disciplining favored by the TV parents.

Lesson: Read selections from Sirach and Proverbs presenting advice for proper parenting and discipline.

Follow-up: Reflect upon the parenting you experienced as a youngster, and the customs you follow or plan to follow in your own family.

PREPARATION

To stimulate interest and a particular focus for this lesson, try to watch one or several different TV programs focused on family. Observe the methods of parenting and disciplining favored by the TV parents in programs such as "Who's the Boss?" "Roseanne," "The Wonder Years," "The Cosby Show," "Mr. Belvedere," among others. Compare what is seen in these fictional stories with personal, real-life experience.

Background

Contemporary western experts on parenting and discipline observe that a parent must seek to balance parental authority with a child's need to develop autonomy. In a democratic society such as the United States, parenting is considered most effective if it is based upon principles of freedom, justice, and equality for all. Parents encourage and respect the freedom of their children, strive to be fair with their children, and seek to treat all their children equally.

Here are some general methods by which this kind of parenting is carried out:

A. Modeling. It is believed that western youngsters adopt life-styles by observing and imitating the life-styles of adults they admire: their parents, heroes and heroines, and often even villains. Technically this is called "observational learning." In a culture that believes this to be a good strategy for parenting, all adults must strive to model the behavior, attitudes, and values they would like youngsters to accept and adopt. And the most effective modeling is accompanied by reinforcement which takes place through rewards, but better yet when the youngsters realize the pleasant consequences of the behaviors, attitudes and values they are imitating.

In the TV program(s) you have analyzed, are the parents and adults conscious of the need to model appropriate behavior, attitudes and values?

What do sensitive adults do when they become aware of personally failing to model appropriate behavior for youngsters?

How do responsible adults explain or discourage the undesirable life-styles, behaviors, attitudes, and values their youngsters might observe in some adults (relatives, neighbors, or others)?

B. Stimulating good behavior through a series of rewards or reinforcements. This parenting process is called *behavior modification* because it seeks to increase a child's desirable behaviors by reinforcing them and to discourage undesirable behaviors by ignoring them.

First a parent "observes" the child's behavior. Sometimes this alone stimulates a child to behave appropriately—Americans do not like "being watched." If this doesn't work, the next step is to sit down with the youngsters and specify or pinpoint the undesirable behaviors that have been observed. After an undesirable behavior has been identified for the youngsters, the parent will "ignore" these behaviors while rewarding the good behaviors (with candy, toys, hug, wink, smile, word of praise) when they occur. (Perhaps a better word than "ignore" is "refuse to reward," for instance, by noticing them, relating to them, or giving in to them—all of which actions would be interpreted by the misbehaving child as a "reward" for bad behavior.) The final step is evaluation—a return to "observation" as it were, to focus on newly emerging undesirable behaviors.

It is believed that this method of parenting does

away with punishment. Clearly this method is limited to behaviors, values, and attitudes whose consequences can be temporarily disregarded. Those undesirable behaviors which have damaging consequences need to be treated differently and immediately!

A fairly frequent behavior-modification strategy of a bygone era was a spanking. Do TV parents ever resort to spanking? Do contemporary real-life parents ever resort to spanking? How is spanking explained, understood, and practiced today as a strategy for modifying the undesirable behavior of growing youngsters?

C. Cognitive Approaches. This method requires that a parent tailor a child's guidance according to the stage of cognitive development that the child has reached. In simplest form, this method believes "experience is the best teacher." Children must be permitted to test various responses to a variety of situations and to learn from their own experiences which behavior is encouraged and which is inappropriate. In this way, they will be able to develop *their own inner* controls.

With this method, the parent must be very specific by laying down limits of behavior and spelling out the consequences of breaking these limits. In addition, the parent must give the child some idea of what kind of acceptable behavior is expected.

When a youngster is angry or upset, the prudent parent prevents that child from hurting self, others, or property. After the feeling passes, then a good talk with the child can help expand the youngster's understanding.

Do any TV or real-life parents familiar to you utilize any of the parenting strategies briefly described above?

Have strategies other than the ones mentioned occurred to you?

Is punishment a common strategy for managing undesirable behaviors, attitudes and values?

What forms does this punishment take and how does it work?

This reflection upon fictional parenting scenarios presented in TV shows and the real-life parenting strategies utilized by participants in this study-program sets the stage for understanding the contrasting parenting strategies proposed by the sages of the ancient Mediterranean world.

LESSON: Parenting and Physical Discipline

Here is a model illustrating contrasting models of child-rearing or parenting.

MODEL OF TRUSTING, COOPERATIVE STYLE OF PARENTING "TV FAMILIES"	MODEL OF DISTRUSTFUL AND DIRECTIVE STYLE OF PARENTING Sirach 30
• Basic attitude: trust and acceptance of child and its biological needs	• Basic attitude: distrust and non-acceptance toward child and its biological needs
• Parents' perception: child is immature and dependent: wants as much satisfaction and gratification as it needs ("an adequate supply")	• Parents' perception: child is selfish and demanding: wants as much satisfaction and gratification as it can get ("probably too much")

- To obtain this gratification/ satisfaction: child responds to its mechanisms which assures its needs will be met

- Gratification leads to satisfaction and contentment; no worry about "spoiling"

Parenting Style:

- Parent seeks a good relationship with the child

- Parents and child develop together

- Child's capacity for self-regulation is developed

- Teach child to avoid common dangers

- Parents seek to understand child's point of view; in their requests, they consider child's feelings and capacities; child's feelings are accepted (though options of authority and force are available when needed)

- Result: mutually satisfying interpersonal relationships between parents and children; joy and delight; emotional maturation facilitated.

- To obtain this gratification/ satisfaction: child becomes manipulative, cunning, demanding, and self-willed

- Gratification leads to "spoiling" if more than enough is given

Parenting Style:

- Parent seeks to control and direct the child

- Child must conform to a pre-determined pattern

- Child must learn to accept authority and discipline

- Teach child right from wrong

- Parents often ignore child's point of view; in their requests, they disregard child's feelings and capacities; hostility and negativity are aggravated, and unless repressed, they require force to control

- Result: increased risk of conflict, frustration, and stress in unsatisfying relationships; emotional maturity at risk; maladjustment and psychopathology.

Chart patterned after Peter S. Cook, "Childrearing, Culture and Mental Health: Exploring an Ethological-Evolutionary Perspective in Child Psychiatry and Preventive Mental Health with Particular References to Two Contrasting Approaches to Early Childrearing," in *The Medical Journal of Australia Special Supplement* 2 (1978) 8.

The "trusting, cooperative" style of parenting is exemplified by "Parent-Effectiveness Training" programs. It is familiar to mainstream U.S. television viewers in most family-based programs shown in the U.S. The "Bill Cosby Show," featuring the fictional "Huxtable" family, is an excellent example of this style.

The "basic distrust" model of childrearing or parenting is called such because it stems from a basic attitude of distrust toward the youngster and its essential biological needs, combined with a correlative belief in the necessity of directive child-rearing techniques. In general, this model characterizes parenting styles widespread in the ancient Mediterranean world. Consider the advice offered by Sirach and Proverbs.

READ Sirach 30:1–13. Take special note of verses 1 and 12.

30:1

30:12

As one biblical commentator notes: "The physical punishment of children was taken for granted in Israelite society." Sirach confidently affirms: "Lashes and discipline are at all times wisdom" (22:6). From your own reading of the book of Proverbs, you might recall the number of "wise sayings" that encouraged such physical discipline for children.

CONSULT and take note of the following proverbs:

Proverbs 13:24

Proverbs 19:18

Proverbs 22:15

Proverbs 23:13–14

Proverbs 29:15

Proverbs 29:17

Proverbs 29:19

The advice of these proverbs is directly opposed to the principles commonly accepted by the majority of contemporary American parents. In fact, these instructions sound violent and repulsive. Most Americans would probably say such strategies would be counter-productive. Why are they in the Bible at all?

Recall the advice of Vatican II presented in session one, that interpreters of the Bible must pay careful attention to the culture of the biblical authors and their culturally peculiar ways of perceiving reality.

Background

Parenting in the Mediterranean world is a value by which adults socialize their children to be loyal to their family of origin. This group loyalty is the cement that keeps the family together, and it doesn't come naturally. It has to be inculcated from early childhood. Such loyalty is clearly related very intimately to the core Mediterranean values of honor and shame because these values are primarily group values. Recall that individual members share in the honor of the family, the group, and one member's misbehavior shames the entire group.

Since the cornerstone of Mediterranean families is the father, children are taught at an early age to submit their wills to the authority of the father and/or the actual male head of the family.

Note 3:6–7:

How is a child expected to serve parents?

READ 1 Timothy 3:2, 4.

How ought the best candidate for the office of elder treat personal children?

READ and ponder very carefully Hebrews 12:7–11.

How is the behavior of God like the behavior of a father?

What is the long-term benefit of physical discipline?

What is your response to this passage?

The honor of a father, elder, patriarch depends to a very great extent upon his being able to impose his will upon the members of the entire family. This kind of loyal and obedient family is strong and united when the challenge arises to defend family interests against other competing families. In the village, such a family can be counted on to represent the larger community in *external* relationships. Clearly a patriarch must use strong discipline to ensure such intense loyalty.

Girls

Notice that most of the advice in Sirach and Proverbs concerns "sons" or is addressed to boys. Sirach wrote his book exclusively for young men who lived in a male-oriented and male-dominated society. He had no intention of instructing women.

The instruction that was part of a girl's upbringing came from her mother and the other women who as early as possible in a young girl's life began to teach her what was expected of her. The women also taught the strategies for living within these harsh expectations. For this reason, Sirach is concerned with how much time a young girl spends among married women.

He gives the reason for this in Sirach 42:11:

Girls were treated harshly in their youth and socialized as soon as possible to adopt the lifelong female roles expected of them. In effect, Mediterranean girls have no childhood. They must assume domestic and other feminine tasks as soon as they are capable. Their customary tasks in this culture are difficult and physically demanding.

In addition, they are taught to be subordinate.

How does Sirach view unruliness? READ Sirach 22:3.

An unruly daughter is one who is disobedient and insubordinate to males: father, brothers, husband. The husband could legitimately send an insubordinate wife back to her father, who would then be expected to return the bride-price, the money a husband's family paid to the bride's family for "removing" (as it were) an economic asset from their household. Given the subsistence economy in which peasants lived, unruly and insubordinate daughters could thus ruin a father and the family.

A young girl who is not appropriately disciplined thus becomes an unruly, shameless, hussy who shames both father and husband and is despised by both (see Sirach 22:3–5).

READ Sirach's additional advice in 42:11.

What are three possible outcomes of neglecting to discipline a headstrong daughter?

In the NT this feminine value of subordination is echoed in the instruction offered by 1 Timothy 2:11:

The young girl is explicitly taught that a woman is of little value.

READ Sirach 25:24.

Is this your understanding of "how it all began"?

In the final analysis, a woman is expected to remain always subservient to men.

READ Sirach 9:2:

and compare Ephesians 5:22:

A father has no role in parenting any children until puberty, and then his chief focus is his son. But his daughters are viewed as posing lifelong problems.

READ Sirach 42:9–10, and write down the six concerns that keep a father awake at night:

1.

2.

3.

4.

5.

6.

Perceptive readers will notice that this entire passage reflects a Mediterranean father's concern for his honor which is directly affected by his daughters who in the ways listed here are culturally perceived as shaming the father and family. (Recall session two on the core Mediterranean values of honor and shame, and the key role played by women in the family's honor.)

In summary, the parenting of Mediterranean girls is done by the women who see their task as preparing a young girl to assume the proper honorable status in society.

Pause at this point to ponder, and if possible, to discuss:

Are any (1) modeling (2) behavior modification or (3) cognitive strategies evident in these biblical passages?

For example, do the women parent young girls only by talking to them?

– by modeling examples of suitable behavior?

– by rewarding good behaviors and penalizing undesirable behaviors?

Are youngsters believed to pass through stages of development in the ancient Mediterranean world?

If you have identified modeling, behavior modification, or cognitive strategies, how and why do they differ from those commonly promoted in our modern western world?

Boys

Boys, in contrast to girls, lead a pampered youth. As infants and young children, boys are reared exclusively by all the women-kin and live in the women's company. They are pampered at every turn. Boys are breast-fed twice as long as girls are, until long after they can speak. Hannah first weaned her son when he was old enough to remain at Shiloh and minister to the Lord with Eli the priest and his sons (READ 1 Samuel 1:12–18; 2:11). A young boy simply has to say "milk" and he is immediately fed. He soon perceives that his every spoken word is a command to the women who immediately serve him. It is not difficult to imagine a boy who has been brought up like this to become an author in his adult years and write Genesis 1 where God causes everything to happen just by saying a word.

At puberty, the boy must move from the warm and comfortable world of the women into the harsh, authoritarian, strictly hierarchically-ordered male world. The recommendation of physical punishment of sons given by Sirach on the proper upbringing of sons illustrates this severity. Let us return to the poems in Sirach 30 cited at the beginning of this lesson.

Sirach 30:1–6, 7–13

The first poem (1–6) highlights the *benefits* reaped by a father from physically disciplining his son(s).

1. The father will find joy when his well-disciplined son grows up. Such a son will provide material support and assistance in conflict with other families ("benefit"), allowing the patriarch of a victorious family to "boast" among his intimates, perhaps among the very ones his son has helped to best in the never-ending cultural game of augmenting honor and shaming those outside the family.

2. Education, it must be remembered, was hands-on and

practical. The son was expected to take up his father's trade or profession. The father's enemy in this context may well have been an occupational competitor whose son did not dutifully take up his father's profession. Clearly such an enemy would feel shame; the friends with whom the father shares delight are likely themselves fathers of similarly dutifully obedient sons.

3. Even death does not sadden a father who has successfully parented an obedient and respectful son. Such a son will be, in modern terms, "a spitting image" of the father. Recall Gabael's comment when he sees Tobit's son Tobiah to whom he returns the father's money held in trust:

READ Tobit 9:6 in its entirety.

The honor vocabulary (noble, good, upright, charitable) in this passage makes it evident that Gabael is referring to more than physical resemblance.

4. In the Mediterranean world where strong governmental authority was sometimes lacking, wronged persons relied on the male next-of-kin to punish or extract satisfaction from wrongdoers. Since the wrong shamed a person or, more correctly, that person's group, that person's male next-of-kin was obliged to restore lost honor.

The psalmist describes the situation well:

READ Psalm 127:5.

What kind of imagery is used to describe a good son?

The combative imagery is clear and self-evident. READ Numbers 35 and note very carefully the description of the cities of refuge from the "avenger of blood" who killed someone unintentionally.

READ 2 Samuel 13 and see how David's son Absalom avenged his sister Tamar's shame when the weak father, King David, failed to discipline his incestuous son, Amnon.

In the context of these three passages (Psalm 127; Numbers 25; and 2 Samuel 13), the comment of Sirach takes on fresh meaning: even if a father dies, his well-disciplined son will avenge him against foes, but also after the manner of his father this son will repay friends with generous kindness. The story of Tobit illustrates this very well.

The sad results of failing to discipline one's son in the second poem (vv 7–13) are the "bad news" counterpart to the "good news" of the first poem (vv 1–6).

1. The worst result of inadequate discipline is a stubborn son (vv 8, 12) who will be disobedient and impudent, or worse yet, who may even kill his father.

READ 2 Samuel 17 to realize the real possibility of such impudence.

Recall the discussion of honor and shame in session three that required the *suppression* of culturally inappropriate behavior. Such suppressed behavior can burst out unexpectedly (a common occurrence in Middle-Eastern cultures), but strong physical discipline can reinforce the need for the individual to continually suppress such behavior.

READ Deuteronomy 21:18–21 to learn the severe penalties permitted by the Torah for a stubborn, unruly, and disobedient son.

2. Notice the caution against pampering, indulging or sharing in the son's frivolity (vv 9–11). This advice pertains to post-pubescent boys because pampering and indulgence are normal parenting strategies for infant and pre-pubescent boys. Some readers might point to Proverbs 22:6 as an expression of a rule for "positive" parenting:

> Train up a child in a way he should go,
> and when he is old he will not depart from it.

The Hebrew word translated "train up" derives from the word for "palate." The dictionary suggests that this meaning is related to the practice of rubbing a youngster's palate with chewed dates. Other cultures have similar practices intending that a child associate a sweet or bitter taste with a sweet or bitter experience. In the case of pre-pubescent boys, this practice seems to serve but one purpose: to fit into the overall pattern of pampering that is reserved for male children.

In regard to post-pubescent boys, it is obviously not likely that an adult could literally rub the palates of these grown boys with chewed dates, yet the comparison of wisdom to honey (READ Sirach 24:20) and the repeated encouragement that the post-pubescent boy seek wisdom should be seen less as a "positive" exhortation to desirable behavior than as a description of the results of being submissive, obedient, and dutiful toward the father.
To test this out,

READ Sirach 7:23.

Or for an alternative expression of the same thought,

READ Sirach 22:2.

In actuality, instruction and wisdom are not always appealing in themselves.

READ Sirach 6:20–21.

This is why physical coercion in the form of physical discipline is necessary. And the post-pubescent boy who refuses to learn wisdom from his father and other adult males in his world can expect severe and bitter physical punishment.

Initially, of course, early after the boy has been pushed out of the women's world into the men's world, the shock of such discipline is great. Boys run back to the women who now, however, must send them back to the men's world. The stern, severe, authoritarian ways of the older men, especially the father, leave a strong if painful impression on the young boy. And it takes years for the boy to make the transition from the women's world to the men's world.

Obviously one reason that Sirach, Proverbs, and other sections of the Mediterranean-produced Bible unhesitatingly prescribe physical discipline is to help the pubescent boy realize that he is not a girl but a boy, and that he must strive to discover his masculine identity (having had no role-model until now) which in large measure will be proven by his ability to bear pain unflinchingly and in silence. It will require a lot of effort to redirect the orientation begun by the women-kin.

The corollary to such an approach to parenting is evident. The father will administer physical discipline in the belief that it will not only train the youngster well to be a man, but will also inure him to the pain that he can expect for the rest of his life. From the young man's perspective, it becomes clear that the men of his culture consider only such who can endure pain as authentically and unquestioningly male.

The Hebrew Bible highly praises men like these.

Examples are perhaps more familiar than any reader realizes. Consider these passages in their fuller context describing a Suffering Servant (in addition to the suffering, note also the shame vocabulary):

READ Isaiah 42:2

Isaiah 50:6

Isaiah 53:3

Isaiah 53:7

The Mediterranean cultural strategies of parenting and disciplining young boys reflected in Proverbs and Sirach help a reader understand these "Suffering Servant" songs in Isaiah. They describe a cultural hero who is admired, envied, and would gladly be imitated.

READ the Lamentations of Jeremiah 3, and particularly this passage (the speaker in this passage is the city of Jerusalem):

Lamentations 1:12

Similar statements by other biblical persons lead one to think that this attitude toward suffering might be a Mediterranean cultural trait.

READ 2 Corinthians 11:21–30.

Have you ever met a person like Paul who enjoys boasting of his sufferings? Or who believes no one has suffered as much as he has?

READ these gospel passages:

Mark 8:34—9:1

In Mediterranean culture, according to the insights of this chapter and the biblical passages you have already consulted, is this advice from Jesus shocking or something that would be considered normal and customary?

Mark 14:36

In what kind of cultural scenario would a father design such a destiny for his son?

In what kind of cultural scenario would a son respond with obedient resignation to this kind of destiny determined by his father?

Finally, READ Hebrews 5:7–10.

Would this parenting strategy be familiar in the United States?

With regard to these passages about rearing boys, are any (1) modeling (2) behavior modification or (3) cognitive strategies evident in these passages? For instance, do the men train the young only by reasoning with them? Do men (heroes) model examples of suitable, desirable, culturally applauded behavior? What are the rewards of good behavior (or whose honor is increased by good behavior)? Who penalizes culturally undesirable behaviors and how? Are young boys believed to pass through stages of development in the ancient Mediterranean world?

Think of some famous fathers and sons in the Bible. Does this session help you to understand their relationships? For instance,

READ Genesis 22.

Do the parenting strategies described in this session help you to understand why Abraham did not object to God's request? Was Isaac blind, dumb, paralyzed or otherwise impaired not to have realized what was afoot and flee to save his life? Or do we see the dutiful son produced by the parenting strategies recommended by Sirach and Proverbs? Since all theology is based upon human experience, does the Mediterranean experience of parenting facilitate understanding this Mediterranean idea of God exhibited in Genesis 22?

Now if you have identified modeling, behavior modification, or cognitive strategies for training young boys in Sirach, Proverbs or other parts of the Bible, how and why do they differ from those commonly promoted for training young boys in our modern western world?

Conclusion to the lesson

The commandment to "Honor your father and your mother, that your days may be long in the land which the Lord your God gave you" (Exodus 20:12) definitely includes the complex of ideas discussed here: submitting one's will in unquestioning obedience to the father's will, and learning to endure without complaint whatever physical punishment the father and other adult men mete out.

FOLLOW-UP

1. Conservative Bible scholar Jay E. Adams (*Competent to Counsel;* and *The Use of the Scriptures in Counseling*) represents some who take the Bible's instructions literally and who distrust modern strategies for parenting. Ministers trained in modern psychotherapeutic thinking, he believes, would consider spanking as a final desperate measure, to be used in discipline only after all else has failed.

Adams believes that spanking is exactly what is needed. He identifies it as a "vital biblical disciplinary method." His advice to parents of misbehaving children is rigid application of Proverbs 22:15 (the rod of discipline) along with Proverbs 29:15 (rod and *reproof,* that is, confronting the child with his sin and the need for redemptive change).

In response to another conservative Christian who sees in Proverbs 23:7 the recommendation that people be taught to coordinate their speech and deeds with their thoughts (in other words, that they should realize *the reasons* behind appropriate behavior) Adams observes: "It does not take a prophet to predict the consequences of that approach."

Does any advice from session one (principles of interpretation) help you understand Adams and the very different approach adopted in this study program?

How relevant is the U.S. Bishops' caution against finding in the Bible "all the direct answers for living"?

Does any information from session three (core cultural values) help you to understand why biblical advice is inevitably going to differ with modern advice on almost every given question?

Are modern principles in any way guided by honor and shame, the pivotal values of the Mediterranean world?

Does the high esteem of physical discipline in the Bible as described in session four recommend it to modern western believers?

2. What happens when members of one culture uncritically adopt solutions to common human problems from another culture without adaptation or adjustment?

If you grew up in an immigrant American family, how did the parenting strategies of your family compare with those of other families?

Do you apply these same strategies to the families with which you deal at the present (either your own or those of others)?

Could it be possible that American Catholic parenting strategies initially were transplanted European or Mediterranean Catholic parenting strategies?

Do your Italian, German, Polish, Hispanic, Asian friends utilize different parenting strategies than those you use? Which are best?

3. What lessons or reflections about our not-so-distant, American Catholic past, can be learned from contemporary plays such as: *Sister Mary Ignatius Explains it All For You; Do Patent Leather Shoes Really Shine Up?; Nunsense;* or from the book: *Growing Up Catholic?*

Resources

Christian Parenting. New York/Mahwah: Paulist Press, 1979.
Christian Parenting: The Young Child. New York/Mahwah: Paulist Press, 1979.

Session Five

Human Relationships: U.S. Individualism versus Mediterranean Group Solidarity

A Christian minister in Africa once asked a group of Africans and western (European) missionaries to tell him the main point of the story of Joseph (see Genesis 37–50). The European missionaries, faithful to their European culture, all noted how Joseph, as an *individual, remained faithful to God* no matter what happened to *him.* The Africans, in contrast, observed how Joseph *never forgot his family* no matter how far he travelled away from his homeland or what he had to endure from his brothers.

As you read the Joseph story, what do you see: Joseph, a *rugged-individualist* who can take care of himself no matter what the odds; or Joseph, an irreformable *family-oriented* person who can never forget his family nor ignore their plight no matter what they may have dished out to him?

This lesson will focus on the human behavior and human relationships that flow from the distinctive personality types of mainstream U.S. citizens (individual-centered) and of our Mediterranean ancestors in the faith (group-centered).

> *Preparation:* Reflect upon America's unique sense of individualism.
>
> *Lesson:* Examine biblical passages to realize our ancestors' strong and contrasting sense of group solidarity.
>
> *Follow-up:* Explore the possibility of blending the strength of both perspectives.

PREPARATION: American Individualism

In *Poor Richard's Almanac,* one of Benjamin Franklin's proverbs sums up the American sense of individualism rather well;

God helps those that help themselves.

1. Here is a list contrasting the qualities that experts agree would best describe mainstream U.S. citizens and our Mediterranean ancestors in the faith. Read over the contrasting pairs. Then focus just on the U.S. list to grasp the picture presented. Consider which points match your experience, and which points do not match your experience.

Those who pursue this program in a group setting might consider dividing the group in two, with one part adopting the U.S. characteristics and the other part adopting the Mediterranean characteristics. The groups could attempt to inform each other of their own characteristics, and perhaps even attempt to explain why that group's characteristics are believed to be the "best way to do things."

U.S. CITIZENS	MEDITERRANEANS
Egocentric identity	Group-centric identity
Promote independence	Promote interdependence
See the parts	See the whole
Urge uniqueness	Urge conformity
Seek autonomy from social solidarity	Seek integration into social reality
Primary responsibility to self and individual potential	Primary obligation to others and the development of the group
Group membership results from a renewable contract	Group membership results from one's inherited social and familiar place in society
Behavior is governed by rights and duties specified by one's personal goals	Behavior is dictated by the group's mores and sanctions or the leader's authority
Individual worth is based on individual achievements or individual possessions	Individual worth is rooted in familial status, social position, class, or caste
Status is achieved	Status is ascribed
Achieving and competing are motivational necessities and the norm	Achieving and competing are disruptive to the group
Assert one's own rights	Submit personal rights to the group
Equality is a key value	Hierarchy is the key value
Friendships are functional	Friendships involve long-term loyalties or obligational commitments

Any group is viewed as only a collection of individuals	Any group is viewed as an organismic unit, inextricably interlocked
The individual self is viewed as an entity separate from the physical world and from other persons	The individual self is viewed as organically connected with the physical world and with other persons
Any personal decision is made by the self alone even if it is not in the group's best interests	Any personal decision is made in consultation with the group and often in obedience or deference to its will
Private autonomy	Corporate solidarity
Strong personal identity	Strong familial identity
Self-reliant achievement	Interdependent collaboration
Strong desire to be personally satisfied	Strong desire to be interpersonally satisfying or satisfactory

2. Drawing upon the characteristics listed in the first column, one can describe American individualism in this way. Americans are keenly interested in the individual person. Each person strives to be unique, to be respected as a free being whose right to make personal choices is so sovereign that one can be applauded for swimming against the tide or marching to the beat of a different drummer even if no one else can hear that drummer. The Lone Ranger or the lonesome cowboy are representative folk-heroes.

The driving desire for personal satisfaction and fulfillment leads the typical American to assert personal rights and duties which in large measure are determined by one's personal goals. Nothing had better stand in the way of achieving those goals. Clearly, personal and individual achievements are paramount and constitute the chief measure of personal worth, especially if these achievements also increase one's personal possessions. Those familiar with resumes will recognize that it is precisely this conviction that supports the very idea of a resume.

Such a strong emphasis on individualism colors the kinds of groups that these individuals would form. The individual works always to preserve personal autonomy from social solidarity. Any group (club, support group, neighborhood, church) is viewed only as a collection of individuals who decide to join or not join on the basis of strongly personal terms. Group membership thus hinges on an implicit kind of renewable contract. "So long as I need the group, or the group suits my purposes, I'll stay." In this context, personal decisions are made by the self alone even if they are not in the group's best interests.

3. Discuss with others (family members, co-workers, neighbors) the list of characteristics in #1 and the narrative in #2 just above. Does this describe *your* understanding of American culture? In what ways is your understanding different?

To facilitate the discussion, focus on your varied "group" experiences. Perhaps some of you belong to a group like "Weight Watchers."

Is life-time membership the rule?

How long does one belong?

Why does one join?

What does one owe the group?

Who sets the goals for individual members: the self, or the group?

You might also focus on your *faith-community*.

Is membership in this group adequately characterized by the description in the first column?

Does it differ from the description in the first column?

How?

Perhaps your faith community has ventured into small-group experiences of one or another variety, e.g., Renew discussion groups, Bible-study groups, Basic Christian Communities, the Catechumenate.

Has the venture caught on like wildfire or has it taken much effort to stimulate participation?

How large are the groups?

How many are there?

How long have the groups lasted?

4. Your discussion of American individualism and your experience in groups large and small may lead members of a Bible-study group to observe that, generally speaking, the values cherished by mainstream U.S. citizens constitute an "*isolating* belief system." In other words, American individualism urges each person to be or become independent, self-reliant, to stand on one's own two feet, to develop and defend strong personal opinions, to be one's unique and distinctive self. Excessive dependence upon any group is discouraged and frowned upon.

Consider American family styles. One of the most serious tragedies that can befall a contemporary American family is for an adult child or children to delay or refuse moving out of the parents' home. To get this message across early on in life, youngsters are generally sent to camp, permitted to stay overnight with friends, and given many opportunities to "practice" separating from home without crying. Reflect on your own upbringing, and on the ways contemporary youngsters are raised.

Which qualities in the list above still hold true today?

Which ones would you find not applicable?

Conclusion to the Preparation

The aim of the preparation in this lesson is to become aware of America's culturally extraordinary and unique sense of individualism. It is not shared in this degree by any other culture on this planet. Bible readers must therefore be careful not to impose such individualism on biblical texts. The lesson that follows should help make this clear.

LESSON: Mediterranean Group-Centered Orientation

The following psalms are generally identified as personal laments, or psalms of individual lament. About one-third of the 150 psalms in the Bible are individual laments. In each case, it is quite clear that a single person is speaking. As you read these psalms, the tendency will be to read them as if they were composed by American individualists. After all, "I" figures prominently in each instance. To read them in that way, however, would be a grave mistake. Let us read some and see why they must be interpreted otherwise.

Psalms of Lament: 3; 4; 5–7; 10; 14–53; 17; 22; 25–28; 35–36; 38–39; 40:12–18; 42–43; 51; 52; 54–57; 58; 59; 61; 63–64; 69–71; 77:2–11; 86; 88; 102; 109; 120; 140; 141–143.

For the purpose of this lesson, we shall focus on Psalm 22 at some length.

Overview and division of Psalm 22

Verses 1 to 21 form the actual "lament" section of this psalm in which an individual sufferer experiences a long ordeal of sickness and imprisonment. Fully expecting that God will respond favorably, in verses 22–26 the sufferer "anticipates" a liturgy of thanksgiving in the temple. At a much later time, verses 27–32 are added to further echo the sentiments of thanksgiving in the verses just preceding.

"Title" of the Psalm
In all Bibles, there is a line or two like this one that precedes most of the psalms. These lines provide either (1) instructions for the musicians, (2) information about the literary form, or (3) the identity of a patron or author. Some Bibles include these lines in the numbering of verses (e.g., the Hebrew Bible; the *New American Bible* translation); other Bibles do not include these lines in the

numbering of verses (e.g., the *Revised Standard Version,* the English *Jerusalem Bible*). In this study guide, those verses will *not* be included in the numbering of verses.

The title for Psalm 22—like most psalm titles—provides some of the most obscure information in the Bible. We no longer know the hymns or the melodies referred to; e.g., "according to 'The Hind of the Dawn'"; and it is doubtful that David personally composed this psalm which is attributed to him. From the information contained in Psalm 22, it is difficult to identify any instance in David's life as reported in 1–2 Samuel, when he might have had such experiences and composed this psalm. For this reason and others, Psalm 22 is usually dated to the Exile (587 to 537 B.C.) or shortly afterward, about 500 years after David died!

Author of Psalm 22

We have already noted that David is not the author of this psalm. In fact, the first thing to note about the "Individual" laments (and the psalms in general) is that we *do not know* the identity of the one lamenting! Few if any of these compositions were signed or "copyrighted." The attribution of so many psalms to David (whether or not he actually did compose them) instead of to the actual author is par for the course in a culture that promotes group orientation rather than individualism.

It was enough for the real author to attribute the psalm to David, the first and greatest king of the people from among whom the genuine respective author has arisen. In fact, few individuals in the Bible are identified in the singular and precise way Americans identify themselves. Surely in that day and age there was more than one person named David, Solomon, Abraham, Isaac, Jacob, Joseph, Jeremiah, Isaiah, etc. Just think of how many biblical women you know with the name "Mary."

Conversely, could you imagine any modern-day American composer not signing the new composition, not copyrighting it, not recording it, not making the rounds of the radio and TV talk-shows to promote it, and not caring whether or not it might win a Grammy award? Such pronounced individualism is totally lacking in the Bible. This factor alone should caution the American Bible reader against inserting too much "individualism" into these psalms of "individual" lament.

READ verses 1–2: introductory cry of agony.

The word translated in some Bibles as "groaning" literally means "roaring." It occurs again in verse 14 to describe the sound a lion makes. Mediterranean folk—including men—are very public with emotion and never restrained in showing it. When he cursed the day of his birth, Job (3:24) also roared out his groanings, pouring them forth like water.

Is it common to see American men "roar" in prayer? Where can one see American men "roar"?

READ verses 3–5: statement of faith.

Group-centered orientation. Note well that after this unidentified lamenter begins to plead his case with God in prayer, he reminds God of his ancestors: "our fathers."

Recall (see the chart above) that our Mediterranean ancestors viewed themselves as "organically connected with the physical world" (the lamenter roars like a lion roars) and with other persons ("our fathers"). Recall also that "group membership results from one's inherited social and familial place in society." Whoever this lamenter may be specifically, there is no hesitation in linking self with "David" and with "our fathers." The lamenter makes references to *ascribed status*, that is, status gained quite simply by birth and not by achievement. The lamenter was born into descendence among David's people, the people of the fathers Abraham, Isaac, Jacob, Joseph.

Like others among his people, when he roars to God he fully expects to be heard and answered! (READ the repeated refrain in Psalm 107: 6, 13, 19, 28.) Three times this lamenter repeats: "They [our fathers] trusted" using a Hebrew word that occurs very frequently in the psalms. Indeed this word can also mean "bold" and interestingly enough appears with this meaning in Proverbs 28:1: "The wicked flee when no one pursues, but the righteous are bold (= have trust, are confident) as a lion." So the "roared" prayers are rooted in lion-like boldness. And the boldness derives from belonging to the right group!

READ verses 6–8: the lament.

Group-centered orientation. Though "I" and "me" resound strongly in these verses, the reader must recognize that the faceless lamenter continues to hide his "real self" by identifying with "famous" suffering ancestors. He draws heavily on his ancestor Isaiah for his expressions in these verses. He doesn't hesitate to identify himself with his suffering predecessors. "Fear not, you *worm* Jacob, you men of Israel," said Second Isaiah (41:14; see verse 6 in this psalm).

And later in Chapter 53, Second Isaiah describes the Suffering Servant as having an appearance that was "marred, beyond human semblance" (Isaiah 52:14, = "no man" or "not a man/person" here in verse 6) and as being "despised and rejected by men" (Isaiah 53:3 = "scorned by others and despised by the people" here in verse 6).

The word translated "despised" literally means "shamed." Review the discussion of honor and shame in session three. Remember that honor and shame are "group" values. One has honor because of the group one belongs to, and one's shame affects that group as well. This anonymous lamenter reminds God of his honorable ancestors (= group) and hopes that God will lift the lamenter's (and his group's) shame occasioned by his very visible suffering.

It is difficult to identify these enemies with any precision. Given the content of their taunts, they are quite likely not believers, or if they are believers they are among the (priestly?) elite who would predictably see in the plight of this powerless person no sign of divine pleasure. Still, the unnamed enemies are culturally astute. They know how to add to the shame of the lamenter's predicament. They mock him; laugh at him with an ear-to-ear laugh and "wag their heads." How important to understand sign language! "Wagging the head" is a picture worth a thousand words in this culture. READ Psalm 109:25; 2 Kings 19:21; Jeremiah 18:16.

Another Mediterranean people, Italians, are fully aware of the power of "sign" language performed most often with the hands but using other parts of the body as well.

Imagine an American in this situation. How do you think an American would respond to such mockery and insult? Does any proverb or wise saying come to mind? "Sticks and stones will break my bones, but names will never hurt me!" Still less damage will be done by sign language! The American would likely shrug it off at the least, or retaliate in violence at the worst. Both options are inconceivable in a group-oriented culture where the *opinions* (insults, mockeries, shaming tactics, and sign language) of others are of paramount importance: they can be very damaging or very honoring.

READ verses 9–10: prayer of confidence.

Group-oriented identity. This obscure lamenter continues to emphasize his group identity. He is one of God's people, and that is all that counts. An old custom among Mediterranean peoples involved the father's taking the new-born child and placing it on his knees as a sign of accepting the child as his own. READ Genesis 30:3; 50:23.

In these psalm-verses, the lamenter does not view God as his father even in a metaphorical sense. The pleading lamenter, however, does believe God will behave in "fatherly fashion" and the lamenter is simply striving to reactivate God's special commitment to protect his chosen people, particularly this most needy and unfailingly faithful one ("since my mother bore me you have been my God") at the moment.

READ verse 11: prayer.

Can you feel the deep pain experienced by this group-oriented person who now has to say: "There is none to help"? Neither kinfolk, nor next-of-kin, nor fictive-kin... not a single other person comes to his assistance! In a group-centered culture like that of our Mediterranean ancestors in the faith, this is excruciatingly painful.

READ verses 12–18: lament.

Group-oriented personality. What is clear in these verses is the cause of the lament: persecution by powerful people ("bulls"). Some scholars suggest that "dogs" identifies the persecutors as Gentiles, but this is not certain. (READ Psalm 59:7, 15).

Other scholars think that Israel may be under foreign domination ("dogs"), which is why this psalm is dated to the Exile and is not attributed to David, who was never under foreign domination, or that mercenaries ("dogs") may be doing the dirty work of persecution for a powerful fellow-believer.

Bashan is the northern part of the territory east of the Jordan River, a fertile country known particularly for its forests and pastures and its flocks. READ Deuteronomy 32:14; Ezekiel 39:18; Amos 4:1.

These powerful persecutors may also be wealthy.

The second clear piece of information in these verses is the severity of the lamenter's physiological suffering, but the modern reader does not know whether this resulted from rough treatment (physical persecution) or sickness.

What should be remembered above all is that the lamenter seems to have no supporters, no other human beings (kin, fictive kin) to help him (recall verse 11 above). That fact adds immensely to his suffering. This non-introspective lamenter is *not* sharing the depths of his soul; rather he is sharing externally observable and therefore shameful realities. No one is standing up for him against his persecutors. The effects of this harrowing experience, along with an isolating imprisonment in which his persecutors physically abuse him ("like lions they maul my hands and feet") are now evident on his physical body.

Recall what we noted above that among Mediterranean peoples "friendships involve long-term loyalties or obligational commitments." This lamenter seems to have no human friend, so his trust in God becomes all the more important. At the same time, having no friend puts this lamenter in the same class as the pitiful paralytic in John's gospel (5:6–7) who responds to Jesus' question: "Do you want to be healed?" with "Sir, I have *no one* to put me into the pool when the water stirs. . . . " In this culture, having no friend is worse than paralysis or imprisonment.

The near-death condition of the lamenter is indicated by the fact that the officials are already dividing his garments.

READ verses 19–21: prayer.

Perhaps execution ("sword") is at hand, and the sequence of terms "dog," "lion," "wild oxen," might refer to the executioner as well as the authorities and the chief of state as well. It is reasonable to guess that the lamenter might be a victim of political persecution by an occupying power.

The Hebrew text is often translated "[save] my afflicted soul from horns..." but it is possible and preferable to render the phrase "you have heard me." In this way, verses 19–21 would echo verses 1–5 with three phrases: far off; deliver/save; and answer (or hear). Such a literary strategy of repetition forms an "inclusion," a literary device whereby the similarity of vocabulary in opening and concluding verses signals the author's intention that everything in between be considered a unit. Analogous strategies for signaling a whole unit are used in classical music, the opera, and film.

READ verses 22–26: anticipated liturgy of thanksgiving.

Group-centered prayer of thanksgiving. Though an unknown poor lamenter (notice the singular in verse 24) is now giving public thanks to God in the temple for rescue from adversity, this individual insists on affirming solidarity with the *group:* brothers, the congregation, all children of Jacob, of Israel, and other redeemed poor folk. This anonymous lamenter seeks to reestablish personal bonds with the faith group from which he has been separated through his ordeal.

Take special note of the plural form of the word translated "poor" in verse 26; it will likely not be discernible in English translation, but the Hebrew is definitely plural. The formerly "poor" lamenter (singular, verse 24) expresses felt kindred spirit with others who, like him, temporarily lost status but have now regained it.

Verse 26: "The poor [plural] shall eat and be satisfied" expresses the fact that there is enough food to satisfy hunger among the formerly poor group, indicating they are no longer poor, their poverty has been removed, their temporary lapse from the status into which they were born has been reversed, they have regained their inherited status, and they are now fully reintegrated into the community/group. The common conviction of the ancient Mediterranean world was well-expressed by St. Clement of Alexandria, Seneca, Plutarch, Cicero, and many others: "No person is destitute when it comes to the necessities of life, nor is any person overlooked." If a person was at one time so lacking in necessities that one could "count all my bones" (see verse 17), that was a temporary or passing event. Clearly, this time has passed for this lamenter and other lamenters who have preceded him.

Recall once more the description of our Mediterranean ancestors in the faith proposed above on the chart. The lamenter's quest is for "[re]-integration into the former social reality." The lamenter's "individual worth is rooted in *familial status* ("brethren" even if in the widest sense [v 22]), *social position* ("in the midst of the congregation," presumably in the temple court of the men [v 22]), *class* ("the poor shall eat and be satisfied . . . and they shall no longer be viewed as poor").

Notice also the lamenter's relief and joy because *honor* has been regained: "my praise" = "my honor" in verse 25. The *shameful* condition has been removed: "[God] has not hid his face from the afflicted lamenter." Face is a word from the "honor" vocabulary list. And because honor is a group-focused reality, the honor vocabulary in verses 22–26 underscores the group-oriented dimension that permeates these reflections.

The lamenter is not saying "*I* once was lost but now *I'm* found"; rather, the lamenter notes: "Formerly I was cut off from my group, but now I am back in its midst, an acknowledged full-fledged member in the great congregation. I have also regained my temporarily lost inherited status. I have what I had at birth, no more and no less, as

God intended it to be. The lamenter's sad experience and its fortunate reversal is therefore viewed in verse 23 as an opportunity for group development. (Again consult the list of characteristics above).

READ verses 27–31.

This "second" Song of Thanksgiving (verses 27–31) may well reflect the restored lamenter's ongoing and developing grateful sentiments that resulted from his deliverance. He now summons foreigners ("nations"), the sick-unto-death ("cannot keep self alive"), and even generations yet unborn to become members of his group, the group under God's protection: "Indeed, God takes decisive action! (= he has wrought it)." From beginning to end, this psalm echoes group orientation even as an individual member of the group laments a very personal predicament.

Conclusion to the Lesson

In contrast to the striking *individualism* that characterizes mainstream U.S. culture making it an "isolating belief system," our Mediterranean ancestors in the faith appear to have a "congregating or integrating belief system."

Mediterraneans are socialized to be dependent, especially upon kin, real and fictive, to join or build networks and coalitions, to support and repeat community wisdom, to be no better than anyone else, but rather to strive to be just like others in the group. The primary obligation for such people is toward others as well as toward the development of the group. Anything that would disrupt the group, such as competition for limited goods or striving to be "the best," is culturally forbidden and must be avoided. Personal rights always are sacrificed for the good of the group. While U.S. individuals ceaselessly search for personal fulfillment and satisfaction, Mediterranean group-oriented persons strive to be satisfying and pleasing to others. The individual in Mediterranean culture feels very strongly connected organically with the physical world and with other persons. The group is an organismic unit whose individual members are inextricably interlocked.

For such people, the mere thought of an adult male child even considering moving away from the parental home would be quite horrifying. (Though Jacob fled to preserve his life after cheating his brother Esau [READ Genesis 27:41–45], eventually he felt constrained to return [READ Genesis 31] to that paternal homestead. And recall the joy of the father at the return of his adult, temporarily wayward son [READ Luke 15].)

FOLLOW-UP

1. Take some time to examine other so-called "Psalms of Individual Lament" to further explore the group orientation highlighted in Psalm 22.

Read with the list as guide. Select a psalm or psalms and read them carefully in the light of the list of characteristics descriptive of Mediterranean group orientation presented above. Don't forget to include notions learned from the previous sessions: honor and shame; and physical discipline.

Protestations of innocence. Consider, for example, "protestations of innocence," that is, instances where the lamenter reminds God that personal behavior has been appropriate. For example, CONSULT Psalm 7:3–5; or 17: 1, 3, or 26: 4ff, and others, and notice the "group" setting in which the "individual" claims to be properly behaved. Behavior is always related to groups; it is never viewed in isolation as a strictly private matter, or a matter just between the person and God.

Kin and friends. Psalms 38, 55, 69, and 88 among others identify the troublemakers or the ones who cause the lamenter grief as kinfolk and friends. Unlike Americans who can stand alone against the crowd, meet all foes, and do battle with all enemies, our Mediterranean ancestors in the faith become paralyzed when their most trusted and intimate associates turn out to be disloyal, or worse, betray a friendship or stronger relationship.

As you reflect upon modern political events in the Middle East or in Central America, do these notions of kinship and loyalty seem relevant? Does American individualism stand out?

Strong sense of individualism. Psalms 51 and 52 at first reading sound very individualistic. It is difficult to see the group orientation in them. Yet one must be careful not to read psychological sentiments into compositions deriving from non-introspective people like our ancestors. Look again at these psalms and search carefully for the group orientation. Look especially at the expressions of thanksgiving in them. Will it take place completely in private, or will it be done in public? If the thanksgiving is public, has the difficulty or distress been private? Or is it likely that the entire community knows the sad condition of the individual lamenter whose lot has now changed?

2. Specialists in multicultural or cross-cultural studies often recommend that something of value can be learned from each culture.

If it were possible, what could American individualists teach their group-oriented Mediterranean ancestors in the faith? And what could the group orientation of biblical literature like the Psalms of

Individual Lament teach American individualists? Is a happy balance between these two approaches possible? How would it work?

3. Experts in Mediterranean culture point out that while individual*ism* (especially in the Unites States understanding of the word) is totally lacking in the Bible; there definitely is no lack of individual*ity*. Biblical characters are indeed "characters." David is not Solomon; Joseph is not Abraham; Peter is not John. Even while being conformists and repressing anything that would make one stand out from the group, persons in group-oriented cultures can be versatile and creatively adaptive in many different situations.

Within one's group (= family, village, tribal group) individuality is restricted, but outside the family, village, tribe, a much wider latitude in behavior is possible.

Could this explain why group-centered individuals like lamenters and sufferers make bold to stand out in the temple community as they publicly profess their rescue from adversity and thereby express some individuality?

Could this also explain why outside one's basic group (family, village, tribe) strong personality, firm personal convictions, and idiosyncratic behavior occur?

Does it seem that such individuality is acceptable or permissible so long as it does not threaten family or tradition?

4. The challenge of this program is to avoid remaking others who are culturally different (e.g., our biblical ancestors in the faith) into the image and likeness of the Bible reader who is most likely a mainstream U.S. citizen. This is the mark of a considerate reader, a sensitive person. It is similar to the experience of an American travelling to a foreign country for the first time.

> If you have travelled abroad, do you remember cultural mistakes you unwittingly made?

> Can you recall any misunderstandings or misinterpretations rooted in cultural differences?

> What is meant by the phrase "Ugly American" as applied to overseas travelers?

> Is is possible for a Bible reader to behave like an "Ugly American"?

> How might a person behave like an "Ugly American" in reading Psalms of Individual Lament?

5. Many contemporary American Bible readers refuse to believe that reading the Bible offers any challenge to interpretation at all. They find it relatively easy to understand it as it is in English. In fact, they experience no difficulty at all in discovering its "spiritual sense." They are often not interested in any other sense, especially if it involves serious study. After all, God would not make the Bible difficult to understand.

If you have read the psalms, and particularly the psalms of individual lament, have you found a satisfying "spiritual sense" that is different from the sense proposed in this study session? Can there be more than one sense to a single text? What does Vatican II understand when it urges Bible readers to "investigate what meaning the sacred writer intended to express and actually expressed"? Does an author ever intend more than one sense? How could a reader discover this intention?

Resources

Augsburger, David W. *Pastoral Counseling Across Cultures.* Philadelphia: Westminster, 1986. Chapter Three: "Individualism, Individuality, and Solidarity: A Theology of Humanness," pp. 79–110.

Boadt, Lawrence, C.S.P. *Reading the Old Testament: An Introduction.* New York/Mahwah: Paulist Press, 1984. Chapter 14, "Israelite Worship and Prayer," pp. 266–291.

Kraft, Charles H. *Christianity in Culture: A Study in Dynamic Biblical Theologizing in Cross-Cultural Perspective.* Maryknoll, N.Y.: Orbis, 1981.

Stuhlmueller, Carroll, C.P. *Psalms 1 and 2.* Old Testament Message, 21; Wilmington, DE.: Michael Glazier, 1983.

United States Catholic Conference. *A Family Perspective in Church and Society.* Washington, D.C.: U.S.C.C., 1988.

Session Six

Status and Roles

Reflecting upon her fieldwork among a Bedouin community in the Egyptian Western Desert, Lila Abu-Lughod, an American-born anthropologist of Muslim and Arab heritage, noted:

> In Bedouin society, one can hardly talk about "women" in general. Every woman is a sister, daughter, wife, mother, or aunt, and it is the role and relationship that usually determines how she will be perceived and treated.

This observation is valid throughout the Mediterranean world and helps a Bible reader to understand how women *and men* are generally presented in biblical texts. In other words, status and role play a central role in the Bible's assessment of men and women. Status and role in the Mediterranean world, it will be noticed, are intimately connected with that world's core values: honor and shame. Is is therefore worth spending some time reflecting upon status and role in biblical texts.

Once again we shall focus on Proverbs and Sirach for clues in understanding how our ancestors in the faith perceived men and women in terms of status, and how they divided tasks between men and women in terms of roles. These insights should enable you to read and interpret many stories in the Bible.

Special Note: This session may involve more time than anyone has available. Set and adhere to realistic time limits. Cover the lesson selectively to fit into the time limit. It may be desirable to return to this lesson more than once in order to fully grasp and appreciate this dimension of the culture of our ancestors in the faith.

Preparation: Make a list of gender-specific roles you have observed within family life as well as outside of family life.

Lesson: Examine Proverbs and Sirach to discover the gender-specific roles expected of our ancestors in the faith.

Follow-up: Was liberation from gender-specific roles possible or commendable for our biblical ancestors in the faith? Is it possible or commendable presently for inhabitants of the third world? Is is possible or commendable in mainstream America? How do you compare the similarities and differences here?

PREPARATION: Roles that American Boys and Girls Learn

Here are some basic definitions:

Status refers to a *position* in a social system which is evaluated in terms of what others perceive that position to be. Essentially, status defines *who* a person is: man, woman, farmer, shepherd, artisan, carpenter, etc.

The evaluation of a status is based on:

a. ascribed characteristics: e.g., sex or gender, age, birth, genealogy, physical features;

b. achievement: e.g., marriage, occupation.

Role defines *what* a person is expected *to do* socially on the basis of status. Role, therefore, is a set of normative expectations.

In this session, we want to examine the status and roles that are specific to boys and girls, men and women in United States society and in Mediterranean society.

Some Background

The preponderance of evidence from the studies of cultures all around the world supports two very basic conclusions:

(1) in every society, there are definite and typical behaviors considered appropriate to each gender; and

(2) every society has some division of labor by sex.

For example, food preparation is left predominantly to females in nearly all societies. This does not mean that men in these societies never cook. Often, where women do the majority of food preparation, men are responsible for the preparation of festal and/or sacred meals.

Similarly, child rearing is usually the responsibility of females. Recall from session three that among our Mediterranean ancestors in the faith, women care for all children (boys and girls) until the age of puberty. By that time, young girls have successfully entered the woman's world and assumed many of the tasks they will be expected to do for the rest of their lives as adult women, while boys are shunted into the men's world where they first begin to learn how to act and behave as adult men.

Since it is a good principle of education to begin with what is known, please reflect for a moment upon status and roles in mainstream United States society.

United States Society

Acquired Status

1. Sex or gender

In the United States, what is the general status of women and what is the general status of men? In other words, how are women and men evaluated on the basis of sex or gender?

How do you feel about evaluative phrases such as "the fairer sex," or "the stronger sex"?

Does the United States have laws concerning evaluation or assessment of people on the basis of sex or gender? Does it happen anyway? In what circumstances?

2. Age

In the United States there exists an organization known as the American Association of Retired Persons (AARP). One must be at least 50 years old to join. Why does such an organization exist? Is there an "American Association of Young Persons"? Why or why not?

In other words, in the United States what kind of status or rights and obligations accrue to youth? to middle age? to old age?

Would you agree that the United States seems overwhelmingly to favor youth? Are there laws against abuse of the elderly as there are against abuse of youngsters?

What, then, is the perceived status of an infant, an adolescent, an adult, and a senior citizen?

3. Social Rank

In the United States there appears to be a certain kind of prison or jail for wealthy and/or educated people (minimum security) and a different one for ordinary or poor people, or criminals with a very low educational level. Does social standing in the community have anything to do with the place which serves as a jail for criminals?

In the United States, many local newspapers have a special section featuring pictures and information about members of "high society." What kind of people appear on those pages? Has your picture ever appeared on these pages? Have you ever attended the events reported on these pages?

Summarizing Conclusion

Would you agree that, in general, in the United States, men appear to be valued higher than women? Are youth prized more than the elderly? Are those with wealth and power held in higher esteem than the ordinary people? Whatever your answer to these questions, reflecting on such matters will give you a feeling for acquired or generalized status as it relates to gender, age, and social standing in our society. This will help you see more clearly any differences that might exist in the biblical world.

Achieved Status

Make a list of people who, in our society, have a specific status gained by achievements. For instance, regarding marriage there are husbands, wives, orphans, widows, widowers, divorcés, divorcées. Relative to occupations one might consider police officers, firefighters, trash collectors, postal workers, government employees, political appointees, teachers, politicians, clergy persons, journalists, public officials, judges, attorneys, actors, and so on.

How does society evaluate these statuses? Which are "higher" and which are "lower"?

What kinds of rights and obligations pertain to each of these statuses? For instance, what obligation does an off-duty police officer have to intervene in a crime? Do police officers have any special parking privileges? etc.

Can you identify any "intersections" between *acquired* status (rights and duties flowing from age, gender, or social standing) and *achieved* status (rights and duties flowing from marriage or a specific occupation)?

For example, in Russia, nine out of ten physicians are women; in Poland, four out of five physicians are women. What approximate percentage of physicians in the United States are women?

What do these facts suggest about how different cultures evaluate the status of "physician"? Would it seem that in some cultures, medicine is viewed as a "woman's job" while in other cultures it might be viewed as a "man's job"?

Do the differing evaluations of status in different cultures make any difference to you as a United States citizen?

Roles

1. What kind of behaviors are expected and tolerated of people in each of the specific statuses you considered? For example, how is a truck driver expected to behave? How is a physician, clergy person, or teacher expected to behave?

2. Do you remember the answers to these questions: "What are little girls made of?" and "What are little boys made of?" Girls are made of sugar and spice and everything nice, while boys were made of snakes and snails and puppy dog tails.

Do you think these sayings influenced the way boys and girls were treated?

Did these sayings recommend certain patterns of

behavior or roles that were special to boys and special to girls?

3. Reflect on your personal upbringing at home. Note well whether you were reared in a strong ethnic tradition, or whether you were reared as an "American" girl or boy. Make a note of the "roles" you were trained to fulfill as a "good boy" or "good girl" as well as the family expectations of you as a "good young man" or "good young woman."

Who actually did or helped with the housework; swept and mopped the floors; helped prepare the meals; set and washed the dishes; washed and ironed the clothes; made the beds; cleaned the rooms; mowed the lawn; raked and bagged or burned the leaves; chopped fire-wood; went shopping; repaired leaky faucets; painted rooms?

4. As you watch your favorite TV situation-comedies, make a list of who does what on the family shows. Can you identify any patterns? Are there certain things men do and women do not; or that women do and men do not?

5. Are the roles expected of boys and girls, young men and young women different now from those of ten or twenty years ago? Are the roles you promote with children in your care different from those promoted for youngsters when you were a child? Can you present some examples?

6. Do people disagree about the roles boys and girls, or young men and young women should play?

Conclusion to the Preparation

By way of preparation for this lesson, summarize what you have become aware of regarding status and roles in the United States. Even as you observe that contemporary viewpoints are changing, jot down the prevailing and alternative opinions. When you have completed the summary, turn to the Bible and see what it reveals about status and roles among our ancestors in the faith.

LESSON

In the ancient Mediterranean world, where kinship and politics loom as the major social institutions, *kinship defines most relationships*. And where kinship defines relationships, it *also defines status and specific roles*. This is what anthropologist Abu-Lughod was referring to when she noted that in the culture of the Middle East it is hardly possible to speak about "women in general." Biblical reflections on women (and men) are always targeted at a specific kind of woman or man, often in relationship to acquired or achieved status.

It may already be evident from previous readings of Proverbs and Sirach that the majority of passages are directed at husbands, brothers, sons, wives, sisters, daughters, and the like. Some few passages appear to speak of women or men in general. As you read the passages proposed in this lesson, keep this in mind, for few of them will be as clearly to the point as a modern reader might like them to be. But patience and endurance in searching and reading will be rewarded.

Part One: Status

Recall what was noted above:

Status refers to a *position* in a social system which is evaluated in terms of what *others* perceive that position to be. Essentially, status defines *who* a person is: man, woman, farmer, shepherd, artisan, carpenter, etc.

The evaluation of a status is based on:

a. ascribed characteristics: e.g., sex or gender, age, birth, genealogy, physical features

b. achievement: e.g., marriage, occupation.

Strive to discern the *assessment of status* in the following passages, grouped—insofar as possible—according to achieved characteristics.

Gender:

Here are some biblical passages which pertain to *women* in general. Notice what they also say about wives, sisters, mothers, etc. Read these passages and note carefully what they express or imply about the status of woman. Take special note of the adjectives that describe the woman, or the kinds of successes or failures one might find in women.

READ Sirach 9:3–8

Sirach 19:2–4

Sirach 25:13–26

Proverbs 2:16–19

Proverbs 5:3–6

Proverbs 5:20

Proverbs 6:23–24

Proverbs 7:4–5

Proverbs 9:13–18

Proverbs 21:9–19

Proverbs 22:14

Proverbs 25:24

Proverbs 27:15–16

Proverbs 30:20–23

Proverbs 31:3

In these passages, what kind of status do women in general seem to have in this society?

Do the adjectives describing women in these passages give you some clue about women who have good status or bad status?

By compiling the favorable and unfavorable descriptions of women in these passages into a unit, what is the "ideal" woman this culture admires?

Do women seem to have any "rights" by reason of their status as women? Does their gender include any rights?

How then is the status of women evaluated in this culture?

Passages referring to *men* in general overwhelmingly dominate Sirach and Proverbs. Here are some clusters of passages related to *men* in general. Notice once more how "relationships" dictate a certain status or behavior. Take note of the sentences pertaining to sons, brothers, etc. Some translations use inclusive language and may substitute a word like "person" instead of "man" in these verses. For the sake of this exercise, consider that the verses are describing men only.

READ these two clusters of passages relating to *men in general:*

Sirach 14–23;

Proverbs 10–20.

Notice the adjectives: wise, foolish, intelligent, understanding, hateful, ungracious, sinful, lying, sensible, poor, clever, discreet, stupid, etc. Most of these verses seem to describe a man of low status. By "mirror reading" such passages (that is, turning them into positive statements) what kind of man would have a high status?

Here is an example of "mirror reading":

Blessed is the man who does not "open mouth, insert foot" (Sirach 14:1)

Turning the phrase around or showing it to a mirror, as it were, one would read something like this:

Blessed is the man whose speech brings him no shame.

What kind of composite picture of men can you paint from the information presented in these texts?

Do you understand all the descriptions presented? Where would you turn for help if you didn't understand a description?

Are any men's rights presented? What are they?

Though some "virtuous" men or men of good status are listed, do the texts seem to concentrate on failed obligations?

Age:

Here is a passage with advice for older men and younger men attending a banquet:

Sirach 32:3–6—older men.

Sirach 32:7–10—younger men.

Compare the reflection of Elihu in Job 32:6–10.

Sirach 32:1–2 offers advice for the banquet master, and verses 11–13 present instruction for all guests. Sirach 25:3–6 reflects on aged men.
If you have time, comb through Proverbs for its advice relative to age: young and old.

From these few selected verses in Proverbs and Sirach, what can you deduce about status deriving from youth or age?

Social Rank:

Here are some passages that pertain to social rank. Read them carefully and determine what kind of status (rights and obligations) follow from one's social rank:

Sirach 10:19—11:6

Sirach 26:28—27:3

Sirach 38:24—39:11

What kind of skilled workers or craftworkers are mentioned in these passages?

Can you discern any hierarchical arrangement among the people mentioned?

Is any one of higher status than another (see 38:34)?

Which one is it?

Why do you think that occupation would be considered to have a higher status?

A recent Gallup Poll in the United States listed as the top three trusted professionals: the pharmacist; the physician; the clergy person. How does this compare with the reflections in Sirach?

Conclusion to reflections upon ascribed status (status based on gender, age, social rank):

What kind of composite picture of the status of men and women in general can you draw from the passages you have read?

What do these biblical passages (or others you have studied and read) reveal about ascribed status in terms of age, gender, or social rank?

What do these biblical passages also reveal about achieved status; that is, status based on marriage or occupation among our ancestors in the faith?

Part Two: Roles

Remember: Roles are defined by kinship. In circum-Mediterranean societies where kinship looms as the major social institution, kinship also defines most relationships. Thus, as we noted in the preceding section, the Bible actually says very little about "men" or "women" in general. The reflections are always targeted at a specific kind of man or woman, often in some relationship to other persons.

In reading through Proverbs and Sirach, the reader probably noticed how many passages are directed at or refer to husbands, brothers, sons, wives, sisters, daughters, etc. Where kinship defines relationships, it also defines status and specifies roles. Kinship is also at the heart of honor and shame, for one's honor derives from the kinship group or family into which one is born, or the fictive-kinship group which one joins. (Recall session three on Core Cultural Values.)

READ Judges 11:29–40.

What does Jephthah promise the Lord if the Lord will grant him victory over the Ammonites?

Who is the first person to greet Jephthah upon his return home?

How do you assess Jephthah's daughter's response to her fate? Does she lament the fact she is going to die, or does she rather lament that she will die childless, that she will never be a mother?

What does this reveal about the status of a woman as "virgin" or a woman of marriageable age but who has "never married"?

What does this reveal about the perceived role of women in the Mediterranean world?

Point out how considerations of honor and shame color this story. Does it touch on Jephthah's vow? Does it touch on his daughter's fate to die childless? What else does honor and shame affect?

READ 1 Samuel 1:1 to 2:11.

Elkanah had two wives: Peninnah and Hannah. Peninnah had children, but Hannah had none.

Why is the barren Hannah not at all consoled when her husband says: "Why do you weep...? Am I not more to you than ten sons?"

Does this indicate that women, and society, perceived the status of mother to be higher than the status of wife?

Which seems to be more honorable: the status of wife, or the status of mother?

Moreover, why does Hannah pray for a son rather than settle for any [healthy] child? Does this suggest that the mother of a son is assumed to have a higher status and therefore more honor than the mother of a daughter?

How are these attitudes toward the status of wife, childless wife, and mother similar to or different from attitudes in the United States that are familiar to you?

Some roles in the Bible:

Women

The strongest emotional bond that exists in Middle-Eastern kinship groups is between a mother and her oldest son. It is much stronger than the bond between husband and wife, which is among the weakest of bonds in that culture. Here is a list of passages focused on *Mother*. READ them carefully and analyze them to discover the status and role our biblical ancestors attributed to women as mothers.

Proverbs 6:20

Proverbs 10:1

Proverbs 15:20

Proverbs 19:26

Proverbs 20:20

Proverbs 23:22–35

Proverbs 28:24

Proverbs 29:15

Proverbs 30:11

Proverbs 30:17–18

Proverbs 31:1

Sirach 3:1–16

[Sirach 4:10]

[Sirach 15:2]

Sirach 23:12–15

[Sirach 40:1]

Sirach 41:17

What duties or obligations of a mother appear in these verses?

What rights of a mother are evident?

Is there more advice here for a child than for a mother?

Would one have to "translate" these passages to discover what they might be saying about or to the mother?

Are the mother's rights implied in these verses in any way related to the commandment: "Honor thy father and thy mother"? In other words, does the mother's right to "honor" impose correlative and specific duties upon the children?

If a child does not so "honor" his mother (and/or father), who is shamed? The parents? The child? Everyone? How?

In the light of the preceding discussion of core cultural values (session three) of honor and shame, what does this commandment mean?

Who seems to be the recipient of the advice in these verses from Proverbs and Sirach: boys or girls, sons or daughters? Might this in some way reflect the enormous importance this culture placed on sons and the mother-son relationship?

The correlative role to mother is *wife*. Here are some biblical passages that refer to wives. READ them carefully and jot down what you notice in them.

Proverbs 5:15–19. This advice is directed to a man.

What can he expect from his wife?

Proverbs 6:27–35. More advice for a man relative to a neighbor's wife (adultery).

What kind of "wounds," "dishonor" and "disgrace" does adultery bring to a man?

Do verses 34–35 give any clue?

Now that you are sensitive to the honor and shame culture of our ancestors, what force do the words "dishonor" and "disgrace" carry in this advice?

Proverbs 12:4.

In what way would a wife bring shame, and how would that be like "rottenness in the bones"?

Proverbs 18:22.

In societies like that of the biblical world where marriages were arranged, what does it mean to "find" a wife?

Is there some clue in the remainder of the proverb: a wife is a "good thing," one who is married is "graced"?

Proverbs 19:13–14. This pair of proverbs contrasts an undesirable wife (quarrelsome, like a continual dripping of rain) with a desirable wife (a prudent woman).

What is the contrast between "quarrelsome" and "prudent"?

Is a wife not permitted to "quarrel" with her husband? Why?

Would Mediterranean marriages know anything of modern western spouses' strategy of "fighting fair"?

The word "quarrelling" very likely helps interpret the word "prudent." What then is the behavior of a "prudent" wife?

Proverbs 31:10–31. This poem is an appendix to the entire book of Proverbs, since it is completely separated as an alphabetic acrostic. This means that each verse begins with a successive letter of the Hebrew alphabet from beginning to end.

1. Notice that this poem is appended to the words of King Lemuel (vv 1–9) which he learned from his mother (see verse 1). It is very likely that his mother would have reared her daughters to be the kind of "good wives" this concluding poem describes.

What are the tasks this good wife is expected to do?

Notice that this poem does not describe a particular woman, but rather an "ideal model."

For the picture of an "ideal model" of a man, READ Psalm 112, which is also an "acrostic," that is, alphabetical poem.

2. The fact that this wife has maidens (v 15) does not necessarily reflect a higher social status. Given the extended nature of all biblical families (father with married sons and their families, etc.), and the fact that the house was the woman's domain, a good wife is responsible for the effective management of the members of a household as a working unit. This certainly involves assigning appropriate "tasks for her maidens" in whose number would be junior wives, daughters, nieces, daughters-in-law, and other women. This alone is a full-time job (see verse 27).

3. Notice the emphasis on spinning, weaving, and sewing (READ verses 13, 18, 19, 22, 24). In most cultures of the world, spinning is predominantly and usually, though not exclusively, a feminine activity. The division of tasks by gender appears to be linked to the complexity of a society. For example, in less complex societies women tend to make pots; in more complex societies when crafts become full-time specialties men tend to make pots.

4. The overwhelming majority of tasks mentioned in this poem take place or are related to *inside* the home, the "private domain," usually the woman's special area. But consider verse 16: she inspects a field, buys it, and plants a vineyard. This kind of activity pertains to *outside* the home, the "public domain," usually the men's special area. (Contrast this with Jesus' parable where a man finds a hidden treasure and buys the field in which it is buried [Matthew 13:44]; or the parable in Isaiah 5:1–2 where a man tends the vineyard.)

In general, in the Mediterranean world, this division of the world in male/female, public/private, and similar domains (e.g., clean/unclean; inside/outside; etc.), is fairly consistent because it reflects the ideological underpinning of the culture, namely: honor (male) and shame (female).

How, then, does it happen that the woman in this poem is expected to engage in an activity peculiar to the public, male domain? Evidence indicates that women of extremely high or extremely low status enjoy considerably more freedom in the public domain than the majority of women.

What is the culturally plausible social standing of the woman considered in this poem?

Would you agree that the "ideal" woman being portrayed here represents a higher class of society?

5. Notice two contrasting verses: "With the fruit of her hands" she plants a vineyard (v 16); and "give her the fruit of her hands" (v 31). The reference is to a medium of exchange such as goods or money, and the underlying question here is: "Who controls the products of women's work?"

Is the woman free to use her income as she chooses? Does it become part of the shared household fund? Does it go directly to the husband?

This final verse (v 31) is likely directed to the husband, suggesting that the products of women's work goes to him and he controls this wealth. Verse 16 suggests that the woman, as responsible manager of the household, also must manage its wealth responsibly. She purchases the field for the sake of the household.

The poem doesn't give any indication that the woman here is expected to use her income freely as she chooses.

6. So what's in it for her, then? As with all women in this culture, so too this woman derives her standing and security from the male responsible for her. Her husband trusts her because his wealth continues to increase (v 11). Of course, in this very public society everyone knows about his good fortune, and so his honor is well-known (v 23) especially at the city gate where he spends most of his waking hours among the elders. Her husband as well as her children broadcast her honor publicly (v 28).

> Would you agree that this final poem in the book of Proverbs presents women in a more favorable light than other proverbs which predominantly portray them as dangerous beings who threaten men's lives and fortunes?

7. Among the final sentiments is the author's judgment that the behavior he has prescribed for a "good" wife is God's will: "The woman who fears the Lord [by faithfully fulfilling these duties] is to be praised" (v 30).

Here are representative passages from Sirach. Please READ them carefully, too.

Sirach 7:18–36—focus on verses 19 and 26. The entire passage treats of friends, brothers, wife, servants, cattle, children, parents, priests, the poor, the dead, the sorrowful, and the sick. Could these be considered as part of the extended household?

> Does verse 19 envisage divorce?

Why would a man reject a sensible and charming wife? Does Sirach 9:3–9 give a clue?

Verse 26 needs to be translated in a more positive way: "If you are married, respect your wife."

The second part of the verse flows from the original, negatively-phrased first part "don't abhor or detest" your wife. "If you detest, hate, abhor, your wife, don't trust her."

Leah (Genesis 29:31) is an example of an unloved or hated wife. READ Genesis 29 to review the entire story. The ideal marriage among our ancestors in the faith is between first cousins, especially between a son and his father's brother's daughter; in other words, an uncle's daughter. Jacob has tricked his father and has fled to his mother's brother; that is, his maternal uncle, Laban. A "second best" marriage therefore is "mother's brother's daughter," or maternal cousin, ideally the first-born; here, Leah. Jacob's preference for Rachel notwithstanding, he must accept what Laban determines. After all, marriages are essentially arranged. Thus Laban assigns Leah to Jacob as his first wife, but Jacob does not love her.

Does this explanation help us to understand how a wife might be abhorred, unloved, detested? Remember that all marriages were arranged chiefly with a view to keeping a family nest-egg or patrimony intact. Marrying a partner beyond the proper degrees of relationship would dissipate that patrimony.

READ Deuteronomy 21:15–17.

What kind of provision do these verses make for the rights of an unloved wife and her children? What does this indicate regarding the status of a wife, as well as the status of first-born son?

Sirach 9:1–9—the key advice here is in verse 1: A husband should resist being jealous of his wife, lest she do evil against him.

The word "jealous" carries some heavy freight. God describes himself as a jealous God (READ Deuteronomy 6:14–15; 4:23–24; 5:9; Exodus 34:14) demanding exclusive service, loyalty, and attention.

Since everything human beings think and say about God is rooted in human experience, and all human experience is shaped by culture, God's jealousy surely tells us what Mediterranean human jealousy is about: loyalty, exclusive service and attention.

Now, what kind of experience between a man and a woman would stir the emotion of jealousy in the man? Perhaps the next eight verses give a hint. If the husband is advised not to flirt with female temptation, might his rage have been enkindled by the suspicion or knowledge of his wife's dalliance? In the Mediterranean culture of our ancestors in the faith, women were viewed as oversexed and incapable of controlling themselves. A woman's father, brothers, and husband were obliged to keep a close eye on her, and men were forbidden to stir female sexual proclivity. In other words, they were not to initiate anything.

Moreover, an unfounded suspicion alone could stir jealousy in a man, and that could prove fatal. READ Numbers 5:11–31.

Sirach 25:1—praises the mutual love of husband and wife.

> In the light of the comments above on arranged marriages, as well as Mediterranean men's proclivity toward jealousy and suspicion relative to their women, what kind of value does this verse praise? Would it be easy to accomplish in Mediterranean culture?

Sirach 25:7–11—one commentator has called these verses Sirach's "Ten Beatitudes." Verse 8 praises a marriage with a sensible wife, and laments a polygamous marriage where the women are not sensible but rather give that husband an experience like plowing literally with "a bull and a jackass" combined. (READ the source of this allusion in Deuteronomy 22:10.) An example of such a combination of incompatible wives seems to be indicated in Sirach 37:11a.

Sirach 25:13 to 26:18—reports a cluster of reflections about wicked and virtuous women:

1. Sirach 25:13–26 describes wicked wives. Some translations speak of women in general, but the context (see verse 18 "her husband sighs") makes it clear a wife is being described. (Contrast this with the attitude of the husband in Proverbs 31:23, 28.)

Sirach 25:8 ("ox and donkey"), 26:6 ("wife jealous of another wife"), and 37:11 ("woman and her rival") describe the "heartache" (25:13) of *polygamous* marriages where wives don't get along (recall Leah and Rachel in Genesis 29). Polygamy still existed in Sirach's day.

The worst of "afflictions" is what rival wives do to each other and the husband; the worst of all, "vengeance," is what enemy wives inflict on one another.

Sirach 25:20 is yet another commentary on one possible and unanticipated outcome of arranged marriages.

READ CAREFULLY Sirach 25:22: What does Sirach mean when he says it is great shame and harsh slavery "when a wife supports her husband"?

Doesn't every wife in this culture support her husband by managing the household as Proverbs 31 praises?

Might he be describing a situation where the husband permits the wife to retain the "fruits of her labor" as Proverbs 31 recommends?

What consequences does a husband experience from an evil wife? See Sirach 25:23.

How should the husband handle a wife who does not behave in the appropriately honorable way ("does not walk by your side")? See Sirach 25:25–26.

In summary, this passage in Sirach has described a wicked wife, explained the havoc she wreaks, and suggests to the honorable husband an appropriate remedy.

2. Sirach 26:1–4 describes a virtuous wife.

Does Sirach identify the qualities of such a woman or does he rather describe the effect a virtuous wife has on her husband?

If one is to judge a wife's value on the basis of the husband's reactions, "content in heart, smile upon the face," is it possible that there could exist varieties of virtuous wives?

3. Sirach 26:5–12 returns again to a wicked wife. He describes three kinds of undesirable wives: a "bad" one (v 7), a "drunken" one (vv 8–9), and an "unruly" one (vv 10–12).

How does he characterize each type?

4. Sirach 26:13–18—these verses describe a good wife.

What are the virtues of a good wife? (Look at the adjectives and other descriptors: gracious, thoughtful, careful in speech, disciplined of virtue, modest and chaste.)

Why is "fattening one's husband" considered a good thing?

Deuteronomy 31:20 and Nehemiah 9:5 indicate that growing fat is a sign of God's blessing. Fat also increases a person's weight. The Hebrew word for "glory" also means "weight," so that greater weight means greater glory or honor. In this culture, when a man grows fat his honor is thought to increase, since his weight gain is surely attributable to the household management skills of his wife.

The modesty and chastity praised in verse 15 are significant because women in the Mediterranean world are considered unable to control their sexual yearnings. Notice the relatively graphic description of the wife's beauty in verses 16–18 which echo the imagery found in the Song of Songs. The sense of verse 15, then, is that the husband has done a good job of safeguarding and confining his sexually appealing wife; she has not shamed him.

5. Sirach 26:19–27. Scholars disagree whether these verses are original or a later addition to the text.

Verses 19–21 advise a young man to marry one of his own kind: "from all the land" (= among the Jewish people) "single out a fertile field" (find a wife). The result will be confident assurance that they [understand "heirs"] are "legitimate." (The major fear of a woman's adultery was that a man might lose the ancestral patrimony to an "outsider," a child he has not fathered. READ and compare Sirach 23:22–26.)

Verses 22–27 compare an impious wife and a devout wife. Notice the key phrase in verses 24 and 25: a daughter or wife "with a sense of shame." Recall what was said in the lesson on honor and shame. Observe the keen cultural sensitivity of such a wife: "She will be modest even before her husband" knowing full well he too (like she) is unable to restrain or resist the yearnings of passion when stirred, all the more so when the two are quite alone.

Sirach 33:19–20.

> In light of what you have learned about honor and shame, as well as the role of the father in a family, how do you interpret Sirach's concern that no one ("neither son nor wife nor kindred nor friend") should have "power over you as long as you live"?

> Is this advice related to a concern for safeguarding the supreme and autocratic power of the father of the household?

> Is it wrong to "yield" (see verse 20) this power up because that kind of action would be dishonorable (see verse 23), i.e., shameful for a man?

Sirach 36:26–31. Literally this passage reads: "A woman will accept [as husband] any male, but some women are better wives than others." Some commentators mistakenly view this verse as part of a larger segment whose context is "choices." In the Mediterranean cultural context, however, neither men nor women choose their marriage partners. That is prearranged by the males.

However, as native Mediterranean women scholars point out, this passage is one illustration of the cultural "myth" of male dominance. While men, in fact, decide who the marriage partners of their children will be, women are in the position of controlling decisive information regarding marriage arrangements and often manage to manipulate these arrangements.

In *intra*-family marriages, women's power to manipulate the "arranged" match is reduced but still important, for a female who doesn't like the match can behave in an unfavorable way, perhaps even in collusion with another eligible female who will be the "second" choice.

In marriages that involve a female partner *removed at some geographic distance* or only distantly related, men are completely dependent on the information about prospective brides that women alone can establish and choose to divulge. The rigid segregation of sexes which prevents women from gaining information about the wider society turns out to create the very conditions by which women can exercise far-reaching control over a man's destiny as it is linked to his marriage. It is this exclusive control of relevant information that enables women ever so subtly and informally to determine the decision that men are nominally expected to make.

Sirach 40:18–19, 23. In verses 18–27, Sirach offers a series of ten "better than" proverbs, peaking in the greatest human possession: fear of the Lord. Notice the importance of the "man's" honor in this verse—cattle and orchards contribute to "honor," but even more so a devoted or sensible wife (see verses 19 and 23).

Sirach 41:19–21; 42:6. Again the biblical author returns to the core cultural virtue, this time, shame. Sirach 41:14 to 42:8 describe the "positive aspect of shame" from two viewpoints. Recall that a "positive aspect of shame" means to "have a keen sense of protecting and guarding one's honor." This is expressed in the phrase "be ashamed."

In the first viewpoint, Sirach lists behaviors that manifest a sensitivity to one's honor, that is, things about which one ought to have a heightened sense of shame or embarrassment. These would include allowing oneself to gaze at another man's wife, another woman, or even one's servant girl (Sirach 41:19–21). A sense of shame should inhibit a person from doing these things, for they can easily lead to an actual loss of honor.

In the second viewpoint (42:2–8), Sirach lists behaviors which a sense of shame (explained in 42:1 as a desire to "save face" [preserve honor] or a fear of "losing face" [losing honor] should *not* inhibit. One of these behaviors involves locking one's wife in the home. A trustworthy and reliable homemaker was expected to have the prudence to know how to stay out of trouble and preserve her husband's honor. A foolish wife does not have this prudence or self-restraint and thus needs to have some external restraint placed upon her by her husband to preserve his and the family's honor. Other men might snicker that his wife is not trustworthy, but better to suffer their snickering than lose honor over a wife who brings shame.

Men

Biblical passages that treat of the status and roles of men overlapped many of the verses that treated of women's roles as mothers and wives. READ these select passages relating to men as *husbands:*

Proverbs 7:19

Proverbs 12:4

Proverbs 30:23

Proverbs 31:11

Proverbs 31:33

Proverbs 31:28

Sirach 4:10

Sirach 22:4

Sirach 23:22–23

Sirach 25:1

Sirach 25:18–22

Utilizing the insights from previous lessons as well as the observations already presented in this lesson, READ and reflect upon these passages and summarize the observations you jot down as you review the suggested passages.

The vast majority of passages in Proverbs and Sirach are addressed to "my son" and hence reveal something of the status and role of *fathers*. As time permits, review some of these passages while continuing to jot down your observations.

Conclusion to the Lesson

By the end of this lesson, you may well have a number of charts highlighting the status and roles in the Bible of men and women in general, as well as their status and roles as defined by kinship relationships: husbands, wives, fathers, mothers. These will quite likely be different from the kinds of status and roles familiar from experience in the United States. Perhaps the most significant insight to derive from this lesson is the strong influence that the core cultural values of honor and shame exert on the determination of status and roles in Mediterranean society.

Once again the Bible reader will come to appreciate the cultural gap that separates us from our Mediterranean ancestors in the faith. At the same time, the Bible reader will recognize that it would be inappropriate and erroneous to directly adopt and imitate these biblical models in day-to-day life in the United States.

American Bible readers must accept the challenge of striving to understand their ancestors and discovering the method by which they strove to please God in their own cultural context. Enlightened and inspired by their effort, American Bible readers can then search for new ways to please God in contemporary American culture with a full understanding and appreciation of this culture's potential.

FOLLOW-UP

Reflect upon the following questions:

1. Was liberation from gender-specific roles possible or commendable for our biblical ancestors in the faith?

What has your reading and study of biblical passages indicated?

2. Is such liberation possible or commendable presently for contemporary inhabitants of the Mediterranean world?

When you watch television news reports from the Middle East, what does your newly developing sensitivity perceive?

Do women figure prominently in the newsreel footage, or are they invisible?

What are the roles they appear to be playing in the reports you have viewed?

How much has life in that part of the world changed over the last two to four thousand years?

3. Is it possible or commendable in mainstream United States to imitate contemporary Mediterranean behavior patterns?

Is it possible or commendable in mainstream United States to imitate Mediterranean biblical behavior patterns?

Are your answers to these last two questions the same or different?

If your answers are the same, can you explain why?

If your answers to these last two questions are different, can you explain why?

Resources

Abu-Lughod, Lila. *Veiled Sentiments: Honor and Poetry in a Bedouin Society*. Berkeley: University of California Press, 1986.

Altorki, Soraya, and Camillia Fawzy El-Solh, eds. *Arab Women in the Field; Studying Your Own Society*. Syracuse: University Press, 1989.

Augsburger, David W. *Pastoral Counseling Across Cultures*. Philadelphia: Westminster, 1986. Chapter 7: "Women and Men in Cross-Cultural Therapy: A Theology of Liberation," pp 214–243.

Bourguignon, Erika, et al. *A World of Women; Anthropological Studies in the Societies of the World*. Brooklyn: Praeger, a J.F. Bergin Publishers Book, 1988.

Session Seven

Time: A Chronological Framework of the Old Testament

P hilosophers remind us that "time" is a mental fiction, an invention of the mind, that has some basis in reality. The reality upon which the idea of time is based is "duration." The duration of a person is known as a lifetime. We tend to measure it in years. The duration of events is variously described. The term of a U.S. President currently is four and possibly eight years. The term of a king or queen is usually for life, or until the ruler abdicates or is removed.

In the overview of biblical wisdom literature presented in session two, one piece of "traditional" information about each book of the Bible that was deliberately omitted there was assigning a "date of composition" to each book. For instance, scholars believe the book of Wisdom was written sometime between 100 and 50 B.C.

The reason for delaying this kind of information to this session is that the matter is extremely complex. To begin with, biblical books are not, to borrow a phrase from television newscasting, "live at 5, with film at 11" (or 10, depending on the time zone in which a viewer lives). Moreover, to a large degree, biblical books, just like television newscasts, are *interpretations* rather than factual reports; and of course they all represent hindsight perspective on the persons and events in question.

These considerations, therefore, require that a Bible reader must keep at least two sets of dates in mind:

(1) the approximate date during which Bible events mentioned in a given book took place, and

(2) the approximate date during which written records of these events were gathered into a collection or "book."

While some of the proverbs of Solomon may be traced back to his reign (around 962 to 921 B.C.), other proverbs are earlier, and still others later than these. It would be highly desirable to respect each proverb on its own merits, though the book of Proverbs itself is usually dated sometime after 537 B.C.

This session will provide the Bible reader with a helpful chronological framework for organizing one's biblical knowledge about persons, events, and biblical books. In addition, to continue our exploration of cultural perspectives, this session will explore the biblical world's peculiar Mediterranean understanding of time, which is quite different from a western understanding of time.

Preparation: Time and chronologies

Lesson: A chronological framework for the Old Testament

Follow-up: Taking a new view of time

PREPARATION

1. Suppose you are hosting a foreign-exchange student in your home for a semester. The student will attend a local high school, but you would like to present a thumbnail sketch of American history for this student as a framework in which to insert the historically significant events of your city and state. What dates, persons, and events of American history will you present as a handy outline?

2. An American student spending a year at a university in Spain was asked by a native: "How can you spend four years studying American history? Your country is only two hundred years old!" Would this comment prompt you to modify, reduce, or expand the thumbnail sketch you prepared for question #1?

3. A handy and useful time line into which biblical books, persons, and events of the Old Testament period can be situated may reasonably extend for approximately two thousand years, from 1800 B.C. (Abraham) to the book of Wisdom which was written about 100 B.C., or the beginning of Roman rule in Palestine around 63 B.C. What information would you include on this schematic outline?

LESSON

A chronological sketch of some key persons and events in the history of Israel can help a Bible reader appreciate (1) the time in which the event occurred and (2) the (later) time during which that event was "published" in a specific book of the Bible.

THE OLD TESTAMENT PERIOD: A CHRONOLOGICAL OUTLINE

Part One: David and the Preceding Years

A good place to begin is with King David, who lived and reigned about the year 1000 B.C. David was not the first king of Israel, but he was a very important king especially because of some achievements:

1. He succeeded in gathering together the twelve tribes of Israel into a single, united nation.

2. To solidify this unity, he established a capital city, Jerusalem.

David envisioned a third strategy for cementing the solidarity of the united monarchy and further enhancing Jerusalem as capital city: He planned to build a central place of worship, a temple in the capital. Unfortunately, he did not succeed in this last strategy. That was left to Solomon, one of David's sons.

King David's "History" for the United Monarchy

David also realized that a new, united nation would benefit from sharing a common "story" of how this all came to pass. So he commissioned, as it were, a court historian to write that story. After a while, the historian returned and summarized what he had written: Israelites were slaves in Egypt. God raised up a leader, Moses, who led them from Egypt to the promised land, where David now rules as king.

David liked the story, but said people would wonder how the Israelites became slaves in Egypt. So the court historian returned to the writing desk and some time later returned with the story of the patriarchs. God selected Abraham to establish a new people. Abraham had a son named Isaac, and one of Isaac's sons, Jacob, carried forward the promise of God to Abraham.

Jacob had twelve sons, one of whom, Joseph, ended up in Egypt as a special advisor to the Pharaoh. During a difficult famine, Joseph proved himself a wise counselor, managed to gather his family to himself, and this is how the Jews came to be in Egypt. After many years, a new Pharaoh forgot this story of how the Jews came to Egypt, and enslaved them for public works. This is when God raised up Moses.

David liked this story very much, but said people might wonder why God selected Abraham of all the people on earth to be the special patriarch of this new nation. The story-teller agreed, and returned to the writing desk. After a long while, he came back with a new beginning to the story. God first created Adam and Eve, who disobeyed him. Of their children, Cain murdered his brother Abel. Noah was a righteous man, but his fellow-citizens forgot all about God, causing him to wipe all out but Noah and start all over again, in another time and place, with Abraham.

David liked this three-part story: Adam and Eve and company; Abraham and the patriarchs; and Moses and the Exodus, and promulgated it as the official "history" of his kingdom. The date was about 950 B.C., and modern scholars have called this "historian" the "Yahwist," because his story line calls God by this special name which isn't really known by anyone until God reveals it to Moses!

Thus, the beginning of the sketch of key persons, events, and times in the history of Israel could look something like this:

Abraham		Moses	David	
1800 B.C.		1200 B.C	1000 B.C.	950 B.C. Yahwist

Part Two: Solomon and Subsequent Years to 587 B.C. (Exile)

People and Kingdoms

David was succeeded by his son, Solomon, who ruled from about 962 B.C. to 921 B.C. Solomon was successful in building the temple, and was gifted by God with—and gained a reputation for having—a "wise and discerning mind" (1 Kings 3:12). But his actual life did not reflect this wisdom and discernment. After his death in 921, his kingdom was torn in two by his sons.

The *Northern Kingdom* whose first king was Solomon's son Jeroboam I, was called Israel and lasted from 921 B.C. to 721 B.C., when the Assyrians invaded and destroyed it as a kingdom.

The *Southern Kingdom* was called Judah where Solomon's son Rehoboam was the last king of the united kingdom and first king of Judah in the divided kingdom. This kingdom lasted until 587 B.C. when the Babylonians invaded and conquered the land and the people.

Biblical Literature

Within the time frame of 921 B.C. and 587 B.C., it is possible to insert a few more pieces of information, particularly about parts of the Bible itself. For instance, when the United Monarchy splits into two kingdoms, it makes sense that the Northern Kingdom is hardly likely to recite a "history" that originated in Jerusalem (the south) under King David. Hence, another author called by scholars the "Elohist" compiled an alternative view of the past traditions regarding the patriarchs, etc., and this was promulgated around the year 850 B.C.

When Israel, the Northern Kingdom, fell to the

Assyrians in 721 B.C., refugees to the south took this story with them and it was gradually so well-integrated into the Yahwist's story that it is difficult to separate its strands in the final version.

Judah, the Southern Kingdom, gradually lost its fervor and fidelity to the Lord, and King Josiah in 621 initiated a reform centered around the ["newly discovered"] book of Deuteronomy. Originally written around 650 or 640 B.C., its final edition was completed sometime after 587 B.C.

Schematically, this section of the sketch of key persons, events, and times in the history of Israel could look something like this:

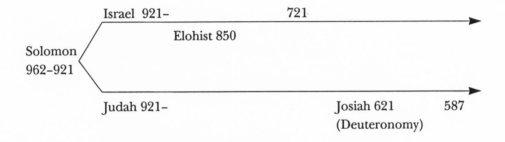

Israel 921–   721

Elohist 850

Solomon
962–921

Judah 921–   Josiah 621   587
                                        (Deuteronomy)

Part Three: The Prophets

The Hebrew Bible contains a section called "The Prophets" and distinguishes two groupings:

Former Prophets: Joshua, Judges, Samuel (1 and 2) and Kings (1 and 2)

and

Latter Prophets: Isaiah, Jeremiah, Ezekiel, the Twelve (Hosea, Joel, Amos, Obadiah, Jonah, Micah, Nahum, Habakkuk, Zephaniah, Haggai, Zechariah, Malachi).

Daniel is placed with the Writings. Catholic Bibles include Daniel in the collection of prophets.

It is helpful to cluster the prophets according to the time frame in which they preached rather than the time frame in which their "books" appeared. Recall that every book of the Bible was composed some considerable period of time after the events it describes. Schematically, then, the prophets can be presented thus:

921 B.C.   587 B.C.

8th century	7th century	6th century	5th century
Amos	Zephaniah	Ezekiel	Malachi
Hosea	Nahum	Isaiah 40–55	Joel
Isaiah 1–39	Habakkuk	Haggai	Obadiah
Micah	Jeremiah	Zechariah	
		Isaiah 56–66	

Two prophets remain to be placed. A prophet named Jonah preached in the eighth century, but the Jonah in the book of Jonah is only very loosely connected with that historical figure. The book of Jonah and the activities of its protagonist are best dated in the late sixth century or beyond. The book of Daniel is not contained among the prophetic books in the Hebrew Bible, but it is considered a prophet's book in the Christian Bible. The book should be dated in the third or second century B.C.

By combining the prophet time line with the time line of the kingdoms just above, a reader can begin to appreciate the historical and political contexts in which individual prophets preached. Pause at this point and do that.

Part Four: The Invasions and Conquests

We have already noted the Assyrian conquest of Israel, the Northern Kingdom, in 721, and the Babylonian conquest of Judah, the Southern Kingdom in 587. The Babylonian conquest was followed by other conquests, depending on which nation gained international power.

Thus the Babylonians were conquered in 537 by Cyrus the Persian. The Persians in turn yielded the stage of world power to Alexander the Great and the Greeks about the year 300.

Alexander died in 323. His victories entailed a worldwide spread of Greek culture that initiated a period of history called the Hellenistic period (300 B.C. to A.D. 300). It was in this period that much of the wisdom literature flourished and also that Jesus and the early Christians lived, and the New Testament was written.

Though the Seleucids of Syria and the Ptolemies of Egypt shared most of the world power after Alexander's death, the next major power to dominate the world was Rome. Its strong influence was already evident in 167 B.C., the time of the Maccabean Revolt, but Rome assumed complete control over Palestine in 63 B.C.

Schematically, this section of the sketch of key persons, events, and times in the history of Israel could look something like this:

Babylonian Exile	Persia	Alexander Greece	Daniel	Rome
587–537 B.C.	537–300 B.C.	300–63 B.C.	167–164 B.C.	63 B.C.

Biblical Literature

A quick glance at the prophet time line reminds the reader that some of the prophets were preaching in relationship to the events and people noted in that specific time frame. To illustrate that point, Daniel has been inserted at 167–164 B.C. on the time line because that book very clearly relates to significant historical events in the entire history of Israel. Indeed, scholars believe that the book itself originated at that time as well. It proclaims itself to be from an older period of time only to give greater credibility to, and gain deeper respect for, its message, not an uncommon tactic in ancient literature.

It is also important to note that the Torah, or first five books of the Bible, were given their final form during the Babylonian Exile. Genesis, Exodus, Leviticus, Numbers, and Deuteronomy were combined into a collection. The final editors, Priests, took the combined stories of the Yahwist and Elohist traditions and added a distinctive framework as well as other special touches. Separate collections like Numbers and Leviticus were also combined.

Conclusion to the Chronological Outline of the Old Testament

Using newsprint or butcher-paper, chart these segments of the time line together to form a handy guide which can assist you, a contemporary western Bible reader, as you read specific portions of the Bible. (Similar charts are available in the atlases listed in the resources at the end of this book.)

THE OLD TESTAMENT PERIOD: AN ALTERNATIVE VIEW

The time line suggested above is one of many similar charts available in almost every study guide, Bible dictionary, or one-volume commentary on the Bible. It should be noted, however, that this chart, as helpful as we believe it to be to us, actually suffers from serious deficiencies.

To begin with, our matter-of-fact assumption that the birth of Jesus forms the dividing point of all history is not shared by all people all over the world. Traditional observant Jews who acknowledge the birth of Jesus follow a calendar which continues to count years forward from the creation of the world over 4,000 years ago. The months of this lunar calendar number twenty-eight days, and every two years a month is repeated in order to match the seasons which are governed by the earth's rotation around the sun.

Muslims follow a calendar that counts time forward from the *Hegira,* the emigration of Muhammad from Mecca to Medina in A.D. 622 on the western calendar. Muslims designate these subsequent years "A.H.," *anno Hegirae,* in the year of the emigration. Islamic years are composed of twelve lunar months and are therefore eleven days shorter than western years of twelve solar months. Consequently, Islamic centuries are shorter by three years.

But to return to our western way of counting time from the birth of Christ—the real problem here is that this way of counting was initiated by a monk, Dionysius Exiguus ("Denny the Dwarf"), in A.D. 525. Dionysius used the letters "A.D." which stand for *"anno domini"* (in the year of the Lord). Unfortunately, as scholars admit, his calculations were not as solid as his piety. On the basis of the calendar he initiated, Jesus was actually born toward the end of the reign of Herod the Great, between 6 B.C. and 4 B.C. when Herod died.

The custom of counting backward from the birth of Christ in a minus series of years called "B.C." (*before Christ)* was very likely introduced by Bossuet in 1681!

Establishing an Old Testament time line on this basis (B.C.–A.D.) fails to heed the challenge of Vatican II to biblical interpreters, non-professional as well as professional, when its *Dogmatic Constitution on Divine Revelation (Dei Verbum,* par. 12) urges that among other things attention should be directed to "the customary and characteristic styles of perceiving . . . at the time of the sacred writer."

Consider the following example from the Bible of how one sacred writer viewed time:

READ 1 Kings 15

1. Judah—1 Kings 15:1–7

Who is the king of Judah?

When did he begin to reign?

What "facts" are reported about this king?

How is the king evaluated?

2. Israel—1 Kings 15:8–11

Who is the king of Israel?

When did he begin to reign?

What "facts" are reported about this king?

How is the king evaluated?

You may want to read further in 1 Kings 15 and into the next chapter of Kings. If you do, continue to jot down what you observe about how the kings are "dated."

Because this program is designed primarily for people living in western cultures, the preceding, western-based time line can continue to be of some help. Some may prefer to identify the years as "B.C.—Before Christ" and "A.D.—*anno Domini,* in the year of our Lord." Others may prefer to identify the same years as "B.C.E.—Before the Common (or Christian) Era" and "C.E.—the Common (or Christian) Era." In the light of the current reflections upon the biblical calculation of time, the question becomes moot. It is, however, strongly recommended that these new Mediterranean cultural considerations be integrated to form a more complete picture.

1. Who wrote Kings?

The person(s) who contributed to the compilation and final edition of the books of Deuteronomy, Joshua, Judges, Samuel, and Kings is called the *Deuteronomic historian.*

2. What is this author's intent or purpose?

This author uses Deuteronomy 12 and 13 as a measuring rod by which to assess whether the rulers of God's people are faithful or unfaithful regarding: (1) worship of Yahweh at a single, central sanctuary, Jerusalem; (2) observance of the prohibition of worshiping foreign gods.

3. Can you find these concerns in the passages cited above?

What did you write in the blank concerning the "evaluation" of the king?

4. What stretch of time (in western terms) is covered in the books of Kings (which begin with David's death and Solomon's accession to the throne, and end with Johoiachin, King of Judah, captive in Babylon)?

5. Is knowledge of this western time frame helpful in interpreting the books of Kings in general, and this passage in particular?

Some Alternative Perspectives on Time

Scholars generally agree that the book of Kings was written at some time during the exile in Babylon (587 to 537 B.C. on the western calendar). In addition to assessing each king in the story line according to Deuteronomy, the author is also recognized as struggling to explain for the readers of his own time and place how they came to be in captivity.

In other words, the biblical author, like all biblical people, is mainly concerned with making sense of his present time: the exile in Babylon.

Duration: The Expansive Present

It is important to keep this present-tense orientation in mind while reading the Bible. It is a very *expansive* present, for it can include a long period preceding as well as following any given moment.

In the person of Johoiachin, the king-in-exile, the author is able to perceive the entire line of kings as far back as it reaches. At the same time, the safe and secure life of this king-in-exile contains within it everything that might be forthcoming from the royal line. All of these ideas are considered by the biblical author as present!

Duration: Social Time

While modern western Bible readers are imbued with "clock and calendar" time, our Mediterranean ancestors in the faith attended rather to social time. Such a view of duration focuses on patterns, orientations, social processes, and the ordering of social life. Social relations and social transactions are paramount. Social time centers on people and transactions with people, not adherence to calendars, clocks, and linear sequences.

This explains the peculiar form that the biblical author utilizes to present the stories of the kings. He presents, for example, the story of one king (Jeroboam) *in relationship to* his competitor in the other kingdom (Azariah). What counts are people, not calendars.

Since this expansive present time of King Johoiachin in exile is the social context in which the biblical author composed this work, the events which western readers would consider "past" are actually present in Johoiachin's person.

How then would you respond to this scholarly opinion:

The author of Kings, who did not use a "B.C. calendar," nevertheless tried to assess the Israelite's experiences from the time they first approached the promised land until the time they were taken from it into Babylonian exile, from the "present viewpoint" of that exile.

For this biblical author, people and their deeds or misdeeds carry more significance than dates on any calendar.

For this biblical author, the *quality of life* in this duration is more important than being able to pinpoint dates on any calendar.

For this biblical author, obedience to Yahweh is the measure by which one counts or evaluates temporal duration.

Consider another biblical author, Sirach.

1. READ Sirach 50:27–29 for a rare example of a biblical author's self-identification.

How does the author identify himself there? What name is given?

2. READ the Prologue to this book, written by the grandson-translator, from Sirach's Hebrew into Greek. Pay special attention to the following:

"When I [the grandson-translator] came to Egypt in the thirty-eighth year of the reign of Euergetes and stayed for some time . . . "

a. Who is Euergetes?

The co-ruler of Egypt (with his brother, Ptolemy VI) from 170 B.C. to 164 B.C. and sole ruler from 145 B.C. to 117 B.C. was Ptolemy Physcon VII Euergetes II. The reigns are reported here in "western" dates, but notice how the grandson "dates" his arrival in Egypt. Is this style of "dating" similar to the report in Kings?

b. Who are the Ptolemies?

"Ptolemy" is the dynastic name of the kings who ruled Egypt after the death of Alexander the Great. A competitive dynasty in Syria, the Seleucids, took turns, as it were, with the Ptolemies in controlling Palestine. Both dynasties were committed to Hellenization, that is, spreading and living the Greek culture.

c. Did it matter at all that the author of Sirach, the

grandfather, lived in Jerusalem, while the translator, the grandson, lived in Egypt?

In other words, what was the impact and "duration" of the victories and policies of Alexander the Great?

For the ambitious and energetic Bible reader, it would be challenging to construct a culturally-sensitive time line segment that would begin with Alexander the Great and move forward to the establishment of Roman rule in Palestine. Along this time line, it would be helpful to situate political events, such as the struggles between the Ptolemaic and Seleucid dynasties and their ongoing tug-of-war over Palestine, and the place of the Maccabees and other groups in these struggles. Then, situating the respective biblical books into this kind of time line would make the picture complete. Of course, the picture should not be marred by western time indicators (except, perhaps, for the beginning or end points), but should rather reflect the measure of duration such as that utilized by Sirach's grandson: "In the thirty-eighth year of the reign of Euergetes..."

CONCLUSION TO THE LESSON

Because we live in the western world, and by its clocks and calendars, and because practically all history and other kinds of books utilize the system of counting years both forward and backward from the birth of Christ (B.C. and A.D.; or B.C.E. and C.E.), it is helpful to master a grasp of basic, important "dates" in biblical history in order to give some solidity to the knowledge we gain.

At the same time, readers who want to be both sensitive and respectful of their ancestors in the faith who produced the Bible will strive to understand and master the peculiar outlook of these same ancestors regarding time. For the most part, the time or "dating" of significant events in the Bible is relational. Everything is reported in relationship to other significant people and events in that present moment. Notice how Matthew recounts the birth of Christ (Matthew 1:18–25), and notice the entirely different set of relational events recounted by Luke for this same event (Luke 2:1–7).

FOLLOW-UP: Taking a "New" View of Biblical Time

Return to session two and its review of the Bible's wisdom books. Perhaps you could select one or another of these books and construct a new, Mediterranean "culturally-sensitive" time line, or one that would contain some "alternative" perspectives on time as they are reflected in each book.

1. *Proverbs.* In the Egyptian court, a certain kind of instruction called *sebayit* was popular. Usually it began with the phrase: "The instruction that A made for B." Pharaoh or another court functionary writes advice for his successor. The instructions cover a broad array of topics that might insure success in diplomatic circles. READ these examples of the influence of this Egyptian instruction in Proverbs. Include: 1:1–19; 2:1–22; 3:1–12; 3:21–35; 4:1–9; 4:10–19; 4:20–27; 5:1–23; 6:20–35; 7:1–27; 22:17—24:22; and 31:1–9.

How would this kind of behavior affect the *quality* of duration? In other words, how would this kind of relationship make time worthwhile? (Note the temporal significance of that last English phrase: a "while" or "moment" that has value or worth.)

Take note of the *durations* expressed or implied in the advice of these passages. Much of it is *present* focused; the future payoff would actually more correctly be called the result that is *forthcoming* from this behavior. The experience of the one giving the advice has validated that same advice to be reliable.

If you detect *future* indications in this advice, are these long-range, far-off, future times, or more likely a period that is *immediately ahead,* as it were?

Some scholars observe that "future" in the modern, western understanding of future, is rare and perhaps absent in the entire Bible. The central and prevailing experience of present time among Mediterranean peasants makes the past and the future "imaginary." Only God knows these durations (past and future), and he reveals these through his prophets. The Hebrew Bible gathers Kings, and the entire Deuteronomic "history," into a section known as the Former Prophets. (The Hebrew language has no word for history.)

These preceding reflections combine insights known heretofore to traditional Bible studies with new insights from an increasing awareness of Mediterranean culture. The reader may find these concepts twisting the mind into new and unfamiliar paths. Patience is highly recommended. The one who would become a respectful reader of the traditions of our Mediterranean ancestors in the faith will need to adopt—at regular intervals—better understandings than those that have been available. It is so in all fields of learning—biblical study is no exception.

2. *Sirach.* READ Sirach 50:1–24, the comments on Simeon, son of Jochanan. The first four verses in particular relate the important deeds of Simeon. What are they?

In the tug-of-war over Palestine between the Egyptian Ptolemies and the Syrian Seleucids, after a long occupation by the Ptolemies, the Syrian Antiochus III the Great (223–187 B.C.) defeated the Egyptian army of Ptolemy V at Panium (later known as Caesarea Philippi) and brought Palestine into the Syrian Empire.

The Jews welcomed this change to Syrian rule, though life under the Egyptians was not harsh. The Jews contributed supplies (including elephants) to Antiochus' army, and even joined Syrian forces in ousting the Egyptian garrison from the citadel of Jerusalem. Antiochus rewarded the Jews with timber for the repair of their temple and exemption from various taxes.

Simeon the High Priest was in charge of the restoration and fortification of the temple precincts.

Would you agree that this reconstruction is one possible explanation for Sirach's praise for Simeon? Seleucid and Ptolemaic rulers both promoted Greek culture vigorously. Under the Ptolemies, Palestine shared in their economic good fortune. Perhaps the good life caused them to take a more kindly look at Greek culture. Sirach, who urged fidelity to the tried and true traditions, might have been glad to be rid of temptations and even gladder to have the temple given greater appeal through reconstruction.

Ultimately, is it more helpful to know the "western" dates, or the *quality of "present" life* under the respective rule of Ptolemies and Seleucids?

Resources

Anderson, B.W. *Understanding the Old Testament.* 4th revised edition; Englewood Cliffs, N.J.: Prentice Hall, 1985.

Boadt, Lawrence, C.S.P. *Reading the Old Testament: An Introduction.* New York/Mahwah: Paulist Press, 1984.

Bright, John. *A History of Israel.* 3rd edition. Philadelphia: Westminster.

Gottwald, Norman K. *The Hebrew Bible: A Socio-Literary Introduction.* Philadelphia: Fortress, 1985.

Hall, Edward T., *The Dance of Life: The Other Dimension of Time.* Garden City: Doubleday & Co., 1983.

Session Eight

Why Believe the Bible?

The preceding sessions have undoubtedly demonstrated that the wisdom literature of the Bible is
unquestionably very down-to-earth, very human,
in fact, very Mediterranean! For that matter, all of the
Bible is very Mediterranean, since that is where it originated and that is the culture from which its human
authors came.

No doubt the probing reader has wondered: If the
Bible is so deeply cast in Mediterranean culture, why
should American believers be interested in it? Why
should Americans care to draw insight or lessons from it?
Why should Americans continue to believe it?

These excellent questions find some basic answers in
traditional theology. American Catholics should believe
in the Bible because it is *inspired* by the Holy Spirit and in
it God *reveals* himself and his will to us. Perhaps you have
heard these words before: "revelation" and "inspiration."
But what do these words mean?

This final session will explore these traditional concepts in the context of cross-cultural communication, an
event that takes place each time an American reader
attempts to understand and interpret the Mediterranean-
derived Bible.

> *Preparation:* Exploring revelation and inspiration
>
> *Lesson:* Spirits and communication in Mediterranean cultures
>
> *Follow-up:* A fresh perspective on revelation and inspiration

PREPARATION

Reflect upon and answer the following questions as a way of recording your current or preliminary understanding of the concepts to be explored in this session.

1. Who wrote the Bible?

2. In writing the Bible, what part did God play? What part did human authors play?

3. How does God communicate with human beings?

4. What do you understand by the word "revelation" as it applies to the Bible?

5. What do you understand by the word "inspiration" as it applies to the Bible?

6. Is the text inspired? Are the authors inspired? Are both inspired?

7. Reflecting on the segments of the wisdom literature read and studied thus far, what in them do you consider to be "inspired" and what "revealed"?

After taking a few minutes to reflect upon and answer these questions, review the first three chapters of the Vatican II *Document on Divine Revelation* to determine whether you might want to revise or complete your responses above in comparison with what Vatican II proposes.

Make a separate list of questions or puzzlements that might remain. Some of these might be answered in the lesson proper. All of them will spark a lively discussion in a group setting.

LESSON: Spirits and Communication in Mediterranean Culture

I. SPIRITS IN THE MEDITERRANEAN WORLDVIEW

Bible readers are familiar with the universe reflected in Genesis: God created the earth; and the heavens above the earth; and the waters about and below the earth. God also created a variety of creatures, many of whom are persons.

The hierarchy of persons and creatures that our Mediterranean ancestors in the faith recognized are:

1. God

2. Gods or sons of God or archangels

3. Lower non-human persons: angels, [spirits], demons

4. Humankind

5. Creatures lower than humankind.

1. God

This hierarchy helped Mediterranean peasants to understand "who's in charge of existence?" The common Mediterranean conviction is that human beings are really not in charge of much, if anything. God and two layers of beings under God are in charge of, and responsible for, everything that humankind experiences.

This conviction stems from the daily living experience of peasants. Farmers recognized that their crops were at the mercy of the elements. The farmer had no control over sun and rain. Some higher power, namely God, did.

READ Psalm 29.

This very ancient psalm was originally a pagan expression of awe at a storm ("voice of the Lord" describes "thunder claps") coming ashore off the Mediterranean.

When Israel accepted the psalm into its repertory, it added the final verse:

> The Lord sits enthroned over the flood;
> The Lord sits enthroned as king for ever.

Who's in charge of storms? God, of course!

Shepherds knew that they had no more control over their flocks than farmers had over their crops. Sheep were vulnerable to raids by other shepherds (fellow human beings), rapacious attacks by wild animals (creatures lower than human beings), or the quirks of the climate (flash floods in a wadi, sparse grazing lands, etc.).

READ Psalm 23.

Do you think a shepherd might be the author of this psalm?

How does this author perceive God? Pay special attention to verse 4.

Moreover, both farmers and shepherds were subject to ruling authorities who could tax their goods and make life difficult. Even among human beings, there is a hierarchy, and some have control over the lives and fates of others.

Nevertheless, all Mediterranean human beings recognized that God was totally in charge of all aspects of their life.

READ Job 1.

Whom does God permit to afflict Job? (See verse 6.)

Are these beings equal to God or subject to God? (See verse 12.)

What does the literal Hebrew phrase in verse 16, "the fire of God' say about God and "nature"? Is God in charge?

What is Job's response to the reports that his entire family has been wiped out in tragic events? (See verse 21.)

Would you respond in this way?

Would anyone you know respond in this way?

Who then does Job believe is in sole charge of existence?

For what kind of people would such a story be plausible and interesting? Would Americans enjoy this story line?

2. Gods, Sons of God, Archangels

As Israel's faith was developing toward monotheism, it still shared with other nations beliefs in *gods* who were in charge of life.

READ Exodus 18. Moses gives his father-in-law, Jethro, a report about what the Lord did to Pharaoh and the Egyptians.

What is Jethro's response? (See verses 10–11.)

How are gods part of the picture?

READ Psalm 86, a prayer for rescue from enemies.

How does the psalmist seek to persuade God to act on his behalf? (See verses 2 and 5, but especially 8 and 10.)

How do gods enter into the picture?

The Hebrew phrase, sons of God, describes creatures who are endowed with god-like qualities. Here are some passages from the Old Testament where the phrase occurs. Determine whether these creatures are viewed by humankind as having some degree of control over human existence.

RECALL Job 1 above.

Who is in the company of sons of God?

What is this creature called?

What do you conclude about the nature of this "gathering"? Are they equal to God or subject to God?

As the story continues, who comes to report back to the Lord? (See Job 2:1.)

Notice Job's response to this additional personal calamity (see Job 2:18). How much is God in charge of?

Does Job have any power over or influence with these creatures whom God permitted to afflict him?

READ Psalm 89, especially verses 5–18. How is the Lord (= Yahweh, God) compared with the sons of gods or heavenly beings (see verses 6–7)?

READ Genesis 6:1–4.

This old fragment of mythology originally intended to explain the *Nephilim* (compare Numbers 13:33; Deuteronomy 2:10–11), human beings of extraordinary stature and power (relative to the storyteller's experience). How are tall and strong people believed to originate?

What does one learn about sons of God from this passage?

The phrase "son(s) of God" in the New Testament, especially as applied to Jesus, brings in a different dimension of this phrase which is beyond the scope of the present lesson. For the moment, it suffices to note that the phrase is a favorable or honorable designation and does link the one to whom it is applied in a special relationship of kinship with the deity.

The term archangel means "a very important angel." It occurs only in the New Testament, and then only twice. See 1 Thessalonians 4:16 and Jude 9. The Old Testament uses terms or phrases that are considered roughly equivalent to archangel:

READ Joshua 5:13–15. Who is the "commander of the army of the Lord"?

READ Daniel 10, especially verses 10 to 14. Who is "Michael, one of the chief princes"? Does Daniel 12:1 give any further clue?

READ Daniel 8:16, 9:21 and Luke 1:19, passages which mention a certain Gabriel. Is there any information in the texts that might suggest this is an archangel?

Finally, READ Tobit 12. How does Raphael describe himself to Tobias?

What conclusion(s) do you draw from these passages in which important angels are mentioned?

Do these angels play an important role in human life?

Do they seem to have a greater degree of control over life than human beings have?

Note: The traditional number of archangels varies. Jewish tradition reckons seven, four, or three; late Christian tradition includes Michael, Raphael, Gabriel and Uriel (see 4 Ezra 4) among the archangels. For present purposes, it is sufficient to note that archangels or special, important angels are higher than human beings in that they know more about the important things in life. They also appear to have more control over these events than humans have.

3. Angels, Spirits, and Demons

Angels are God's messengers. The English word "angel" derives from the Greek, *angelos,* which translates the Hebrew word, *malak,* which means "messenger."

We have already noted the (arch)angels Gabriel, Michael, and Raphael. These are the only angels mentioned by name in the Old Testament.

READ Daniel 7, especially verses 9–10.

How many beings serve the "ancient of days"?

Who are these beings?

Is it fair to say that they are not gods, but rather servants of the one God?

Disembodied spirits is a concept that develops "later" in Jewish thought, that is, a period closer to New Testament times. Many references to such spirits are found in Jewish religious literature from this period which is not included in the Bible. In the Old Testament there are no instances where the word "spirit" appearing by itself, can be interpreted as a supernatural being. In almost all instances where the Hebrew word *ruah* can be translated as "spirit," it means "disposition."

Thus, expressions like a "spirit of jealousy" (Numbers 5:14, 30), "spirit of fornication" (Hosea 4:12; 5:4), and "spirit of uncleanness" (Zechariah 13:2) are not personal identities. They are, rather, "dispositions" just like the "spirit of dizziness" (Isaiah 19:14), "spirit of wisdom"

(Exodus 28:3; Deuteronomy 34:9), or "spirit of counsel and strength" (Isaiah 11:2).

In the New Testament period, it is quite clear that Mediterranean human beings believe in supernatural beings as *distinct disembodied creatures*. Some, for example, are able to possess a person. These beings are called "evil spirits."

READ Mark 1:21–28.

What afflicts the man who calls out to Jesus?

READ Luke 8:1–3.

What kinds of creatures afflict the women who followed in Jesus' company?

Luke has mentioned *demons* understood as spiritual beings, lower than the gods but higher than human beings, who can plague human life. Demons in this sense are not present in the Hebrew Bible. God sends his messengers (angels) to human beings mostly to do good on their behalf, but sometimes to do evil to them.

READ Tobit 3.

What is Sarah's problem?

Who is responsible for Sarah's difficulties?

How is Sarah helped out of the difficulties? (See Tobit 6–8.)

The book of Tobit is not in the Hebrew Bible though it is in the Catholic Bible. Nevertheless, Tobit represents Jewish religious literature which developed closer to New Testament times and reflects a growing belief in demons. The demon mentioned in Tobit appears to have been "borrowed" from Persian mythology which listed this demon as one of seven evil spirits.

In the New Testament world, demons or evil spirits threaten the religious life of the faithful (READ Ephesians 6:12; 1 John 4:1) and they can also work harm upon the human body (READ 2 Corinthians 12:7) but believers understand that their faith in Christ has won the initial victory over the devil and "his angels" and in Christ they have power to resist evil spirits.

Conclusion

Mediterranean human beings, including our ancestors in the faith, recognized that they had little if any control over their lives and life situations. They were at the mercy of God and his creatures (angels and others) who were superior to humans in knowledge as well as strength. These superior spiritual beings populated the entire human environment, listening in on and observing human life, ready to intervene at any moment. Human beings were grateful to receive help and insight from benevolent superior creatures, and as the book of Tobit indicates, human beings also strove to learn ways of restricting the activity and influence of malevolent spiritual beings. But God is over everyone and everything.

II. Deception and Communication in the Mediterranean World

In the everyday world of Mediterranean life, human beings recognize that their social world is part of God's creation and therefore a part of Truth. It is very real, but at the same time, this social world is also in the realm of the apparent, of what is vain and fraudulent. It is the place where human beings play out their lives, and human beings are not reliable or trustworthy.

The Mediterranean understanding of human life involves these contrasts:

Reality	Appearance
What is	What seems
What is revealed	What is concealed
Value	Judgment
Act	Intention

Only God knows reality; human beings can know only appearances. Only God knows what *is*: human beings can know only *what seems to be.*

REVIEW 2 Samuel 16 on how Samuel found the new king that God had selected for Israel. Pay special attention to verse 7.

What does God know?

What does Samuel know?

Since human beings can know only appearances, Mediterranean human beings spend much time learning how to create a good appearance, how to make a good impression. This is a very basic element in the rearing of youngsters. This is all part and parcel of "personality development." People decide what kind of personality they would like others to perceive, and then strive to project that personality.

READ 1 Kings 3.

What does Solomon request of God? (See verse 9.)

How does Solomon manifest that he has this gift? (See verses 16–28.)

What kind of "impression" has Solomon managed to create? (See verse 28.)

How far does this impression extend? (READ 1 Kings 4:29–34.)

What is the "reality" of Solomon's life? (READ 1 Kings 11:1–9.)

In the case of Solomon, what was "revealed" or shown to his subjects, and what was "concealed" or hidden from them in this selection of readings?

READ Mark 8:27–30.

Can Jesus' question be interpreted as a probe of the "impression" he has created on others?

In the light of the present discussion, how do you interpret the various answers given him?

How does the episode end? What is Jesus "manifesting" and what does he want to "conceal"?

Who in this story line knows the "real" Jesus?

1. Personality and honor

Personality and one's honorable reputation are of central importance in this *honor-and-shame society*. Since resources are finite and limited, and peasants have little access to these resources, an honorable reputation and prestigious personality become a person's greatest resource.

So if a peasant has begun life with some family claim to honor, the remainder of the peasant's honor: what that peasant is, the peasant's unique place and reputation, are the peasant's personal creation. Thus, to be born of the lineage of David is to share in that family's honor. But within this Davidic family, each member must develop a personal standing, an honorable reputation.

READ 2 Samuel 5:1–10—What in this passage constitutes some of David's basic honor? How many items can you list?

READ 2 Samuel 13:1–19—David's eldest son, Amnon, had a claim to David's throne. He shared in the honor that David amassed for the family name. What does Amnon's behavior in this chapter do to this honor rating?

2. Deception: a strategy for constructing and maintaining honor

Social-status performances, that is, transactions regarding "personal" honor, take place predominantly with one's friends, those with whom one associates on a regular, that is, daily basis. These "performances" usually deal with one's social standing and the degree to which one "counts" in the everyday world.

The basic ideas are "how one makes oneself out to be" and "being in the know/or not being in the know." Among one's peers, one's day-to-day companions, it is a real art to "make oneself out to be" other than everyone in the group already knows a person to be. The group will wonder: "What's he up to?" "What's he after?"

READ 2 Samuel 13:20–39.

In this very public and very open society, everyone knows how Absalom feels about what happened to Tamar.

READ 2 Samuel 13:20–22.

When Absalom invites David and all the sons to a sheepshearing festival (2 Samuel 13:24), everyone wonders "What's he really up to?"

What does Absalom publicly claim to be up to?

What reason does David give for not joining the feast? (See verse 25.)

Do you think David is sincere or only pretending to resist Absalom's suggestion to allow Amnon to go to the feast? (See verse 26; see also verse 21.)

Do you think any deception is taking place in this story? Who is deceiving whom, and why?

If you could imagine yourself as part of this culture, and found yourself in this situation, whom would you trust?

How in this cultural setting would you make a decision to trust anyone?

READ 2 Samuel 14:28—15:1–6.

How does Absalom manage to return from exile?

On the basis of Absalom's statement in verse 32, what might he conclude by David's action in verse 33?

Do you think David shows himself to be a weak father?

In 15:1–6, what is Absalom up to ?

READ verses 7–12.

What is Absalom up to?

Everyone in the story knows Absalom. People also know when he engages in deception. The various deceptions he projects are the "appearance," and it is rather obvious to everyone. The challenge for all witnesses is to know what he's up to, what he expects to gain. This is the "reality," and Absalom keeps it hidden, sharing it perhaps with some few insiders. Absalom's ability to successfully deceive outsiders about the real "intentions" behind his "acts" raises his honor-standing among his insiders. It strengthens his power.

3. The Consequences of Deception for Communication

Because deception and its related strategies, such as showing off, idle talk, joking, empty words, humorous elaboration, pretense, and the like are such a normal part of daily existence in the honor and shame societies of the Mediterranean, people desperately need to know when others are *not* engaging in deception and lies.

One strategy for assuring listeners that one speaks truth is to use phrases such as "seriously," "believe me," "by my life," "without joking," "by my father's life."

READ Genesis 21:22–34.

What strategy does Abimelech require of Abraham relative to their relationship to guarantee truthful dealings?

READ Genesis 27:1–41.

This is a very familiar story about deception. What is missing in Jacob's exchange with his father, Isaac, that should have tipped Isaac off to the deception? (See verse 24.) What would a proper response be?

READ 2 Samuel 12:1–25.

How does David respond to Nathan's parable? (See verse 5.)

What does David mean by that phrase: "As the Lord lives...."

READ John 3:1–12.

In this discussion with Nicodemus, how many times does Jesus say: "Amen, amen [or "Truly, truly"] I say to you?"

In this discussion, does Jesus say anything about "believing" in close conjunction with his "Amen, amen" statements?

Do you think there might be a connection between these two concerns ("believe"/ "truly, truly, I say")?

Is verse 12 something that might uniquely apply to Nicodemus or could it apply to any other Mediterranean listening to Jesus?

If you read quickly through John's gospel, you will see the phrase "Amen, amen, I say to you" repeated by Jesus about twenty-five times. What have you learned in this lesson so far that would help you explain why Jesus feels constrained to repeat this phrase so often?

Conclusion

In an honor and shame culture, deception and lying are central to preserving honorable status, prestige, and dignity. Honor and shame societies are wide open, everyone knows everything, there can be no secrets. Life could become impossible in such a context. Hence the need to create ambiguities out of unambiguous situations, especially where personal honor is at stake. Thus lying and other kinds of deception are actually "enabling" elements which make social life possible.

God has more knowledge than anyone in this culture, and if God speaks either directly or through messengers, it is important to know he has actually spoken and that the messengers are trustworthy. This is where the notions of "revelation" and "inspiration" enter the picture.

III. REVELATION AND INSPIRATION

Since God is in charge of all human life, and God knows everything, including information of importance to human life, human beings look to God to share this information. When God shares himself and his will with human beings, this is called "revelation." God does this through many means, one of which is to "inspire" certain people with this knowledge or "inspire" them to certain behavior.

1. Revelation

READ 1 Samuel 3:1–4:1.

What does the opening verse state about "how" God tended to reveal himself? (You might look at Jeremiah 1:11–13 for an illustration.)

Why does Samuel fail to realize that he is being given a revelation, an encounter with God? (See verse 7.)

What advice does Eli give to Samuel? (See verse 9.)

What did God tell Samuel about Eli?
(See verses 10–14.)

How did Eli react to the message? (See verse 18.)

Does this response sound familiar? Remember Job?

Who has complete charge over human existence?

Here are some other instances of God sharing himself or some knowledge with human beings:

READ Deuteronomy 29.

Where did Moses get the substance of this speech?

Notice the significant conclusion in verse 29.

READ Amos 3.

What strikes you in verses 7 and 8?

READ 1 Samuel 10:1–13.

What does the prophet Samuel advise King Saul relative to his meeting with the band of prophets? (See verses 6–7.)

A prophet is a spokesperson for God, one who makes God's will known to human beings.

What then happens to King Saul? (See verses 9–13.)

Throughout the Bible, there are many reports of God revealing himself and his will to human beings. These are just a few examples. As you continue to study the Bible, you might note additional instances.

2. Inspiration

Many people in the Bible claimed to speak for God. The difficulty faced by listeners was rooted in the Mediterranean penchant for deception. How can one believe the speaker? Is the speaker trustworthy? Has the speaker ever engaged in the common Mediterranean strategy of deception, lying, joking, uttering idle words? Why believe the speaker now?

READ 1 Kings 22:1–38.

Though this story tells of an alliance between Israel and Judah, and also spells out preparations for war, it is actually a story dealing with the difficulty of discriminating between *authentic* and *inauthentic* prophecy.

Ahab, King of Israel, and Jehoshaphat, King of Judah, strike an alliance to wrest Ramoth-gilead from Syrian hands (see verses 1–4).

At the suggestion of Jehoshaphat, Ahab seeks God's will from the prophets (see verses 5–6).

What is the response of the 400 prophets? (see verses 6 and 10–12).

Why did Jehoshaphat ask for yet another opinion? (See verse 7.) Were some prophets known at times to be "yes-men"? Would they engage in deception to please their "employer"?

What was Ahab's opinion of the prophet Micaiah, son of Imlah? (See verse 8.)

How did Micaiah respond to the messenger's suggestion that he echo the 400? (See verse 13.)

Do you recognize the force of the phrase: "As the Lord lives...." in verse 14?

What does Micaiah tell King Ahab? (See verses 15–18.)

How does Micaiah defend the authenticity of prophecy, and the inauthenticity and unreliability of the 400? (See verses 19–23.)

Who is completely in charge of human affairs in this heavenly scene?

How important is it for Micaiah to claim that he received his revelation in the very presence of God?

How do you think the witnesses evaluated the showdown between the prophets Zedekiah and Micaiah? (See verses 10–12; and verses 24–25.)

How is Micaiah's revelation of God's will confirmed or discredited? (See verses 24–28, especially 28; and complete the story in verses 29–38.)

READ Jeremiah 28.

The Hebrew language had no expression for "false prophet." This occurs first in the Greek translation of the Hebrew scriptures known as the Septuagint, around the year 200 B.C. The translators made a judgment about the text and rendered that judgment explicit in the translation. How would people make such a judgment on the spot, as the prophet spoke?

What does the prophet Hananiah say? (See verses 2–4.)

How does the prophet Jeremiah reply? How can people know the prophet is an authentic spokesperson for God? (See verses 5–9.)

How does Hananiah reply? (See verses 10–11.)

What is the outcome of the story? (See verses 12–17.)

If you could imagine yourself back in this cultural situation, which side would you be on?

READ 2 Timothy 2:14—4:5.

This letter was written in Paul's name after his death by a disciple whom some scholars call "The Pastor." Around A.D. 105–110, this person wrote 1 and 2 Timothy and Titus to two young and troubled communities to defend Paul's reputation and to exhort, encourage, and guide two second-century church leaders and their congregations.

Who are Hymenaeaus and Philetus and what are they doing? (See 2 Timothy 2:14–18.)

What does the Pastor hope for Timothy's opponents? (See 1 Timothy 2:23–26.)

Yet again false teachers are described in 2 Timothy 3:1–9. What stands out in verses 8–9?

The Pastor offers a personal example and a contrast with "evil men and impostors" in 2 Timothy 3:10–13.

Have you noted a pattern of identifying these false teachers as deceivers, unable to know the truth, distorting the truth, impostors, etc.?

Isn't such name-calling normal and to be expected in Mediterranean society?

What then is the Pastor's final exhortation relative to such deception? (See 2 Timothy 3:14–17.)

Verse 16 has become and remains a classic text proclaiming that the Old Testament, the only scripture known to the Pastor, is inspired by God, that is, it is "God-breathed."

All scripture is inspired by God and profitable for teaching for reproof, for correction, and for training in righteousness, that the man of God may be complete, equipped for every good work.

In the total context of Mediterranean culture where deception, lying and similar strategies make truthfulness difficult to gain, and in the specific context of 2 Timothy where the Pastor must caution a young group of believers about the dangers of false teachers, the one trustworthy and reliable fact of a believer's life is that God stands behind the truth as handed on in the scripture and in tradition.

Yes, God can also send lying and deceitful spirits as noted above in this lesson, but his messengers—especially the prophets—make it possible for believers to know the truth God wants them to know.

It may take a while for American readers to grasp and appreciate this fresh cross-cultural perspective on revelation and inspiration. The result, however, will be well worth the efforts. For only then can contemporary Bible readers begin to offer a reasonably plausible answer to the questions posed at the beginning of this session.

If the Bible is so deeply cast in Mediterranean culture, why should American believes be interested in it?

Why should Americans care to draw insight or lessons from these Mediterranean texts?

Why should Americans continue to believe or trust these Mediterranean messages?

The obvious answer is because believers are convinced that the Bible is a special collection of information about how God has manifested himself and his will for human beings. Moreover, in and through this information, God continues to manifest himself. Only serious efforts to grasp the Mediterranean cultural context of this information can produce plausible appropriations and applications for believers in other cultural settings.

This is why Catholics believe the Bible is an important document.

FOLLOW-UP

The deception strategies which are a normal part of Mediterranean culture are not central in contemporary western culture. The western difficulty in reading the Bible is not a suspicion about the truth or falsity of its contents, so much as it is a need to bridge the cultural gap between the Mediterranean and western worlds.

This Bible study program is devoted to bridging that cultural gap. It offers the reader tools for interpreting the Mediterranean texts and challenges the reader to create new interpretations of traditional materials. These new interpretations ought to be more respectful of the heritage our ancestors in the faith have left us, and at the same time be more culturally suitable to other times and places.

With the aid of the fresh insights into revelation and inspiration offered in this session, perhaps the best follow-up is a review of the Vatican II *Document on Divine Revelation*, particularly the chapters that deal explicitly with revelation and inspiration.

Chapter I: Revelation Itself

1. The council fathers note that "God chose to reveal Himself and to make known to us the hidden purpose of his will.... Through this revelation... the invisible God... speaks to human beings as friends" (par. 2).

How does God reveal himself or his will in Proverbs? In Sirach?

Did you identify indications of the "hidden purpose of his will" in the segments of the Bible you have read?

Are these questions easy to answer or are they still rather challenging?

Are these questions important or can they just as well be put aside?

2. God revealed himself in at least three ways: created realities, to our first parents, and through the prophets. (See paragraph 3.)

Can you think of examples?

How did/does God reveal himself in created realities? Can you recall any psalms that suggest this?

What did God reveal of himself to our first parents?

Select one prophet and explore what God revealed of himself and his will for humans through that prophet.

3. "Then, after *speaking* in many places and varied ways through the prophets, God 'last of all in these days has spoken to us by his son' (Hebrews 1:1–2)....we now await no further public revelation before the glorious manifestation of our Lord Jesus Christ." (par. 4)

What are the varied ways in which God spoke?

What language or languages did those to whom God spoke hear?

If we now await no further public revelations, why are people so curious about claims of new apparitions and messages around the world?

Chapter II: The Transmission of Divine Revelation

1. The council fathers assure us that God has guaranteed that what He revealed would "abide perpetually in full integrity and be handed down to all generations." (par. 7)

How do you understand "full integrity"?

Recall from session two that the Hebrew original of Sirach was lost until a *partial* copy was found in Cairo (1896–1900). Other discoveries including some at Qumran and Masada have now yielded about 68 percent of the Hebrew text.

Comparisons with the grandson's Greek translation as well as other translations indicate that this book of the Old Testament is the most complex and difficult one to unravel, since there are obvious differences and deficiencies in each text.

In other words, each verse has to be carefully examined to determine which version has retained the original work of Ben Sirach.

In spite of all these difficulties, Vatican II assures believers that what God has revealed would "abide perpetually in full integrity and be handed down to all generations."

> How would you explain this situation with Ben Sirach? Or, to return to the first question, what does "full integrity" mean?

2. One clue to interpreting the phrase "full integrity" appears later in paragraph 7: "In order to keep the gospel forever whole and alive within the Church, the apostles left bishops as their successors, 'handing over their own teaching role' to them." This is commonly called the magisterium, the teaching office of the church.

> Can you think of any ways in which the bishops have helped preserve and transmit God's revelation in "full integrity"?

> For instance, are bishops the only ones who can give official approval to translations of the Bible?

> Do you recall the United States Bishops' Pastoral Statement on Fundamentalism cited earlier in this study program? Is this statement another example of an attempt to keep the gospel "forever whole and alive within the Church"?

3. Yet another clue to interpreting the phrase "full integrity" appears in paragraph B: that which was handed on includes everything which "contributes to the *holiness of life* and the *increase in faith* of the People of God."

A Bible reader might frequently pause and ask: "How did this book of the Bible, or this biblical author, contribute to the holiness of life or the increase of faith of the People of God in his own time?" That might provide some clues for how the modern reader can discern the value of a given book of the Bible for holiness of contemporary life or increase of faith in contemporary times.

4. These things that are passed down, this "tradition" also develops in the church with the help of the Holy Spirit. "For there is a growth in the understanding of the realities and the words which have been handed down." (See paragraph 8.) One of the ways in which this happens is "through the contemplation and study made by believers."

> How has Bible study so far helped you to grow in understanding of the realities and the words which have been handed down?

> Can you think of any illustrations from the session just ending?

> Are the explanations of inspiration and revelation offered here a small contribution to the development of the "tradition" in the church?

Chapter III: The Divine Inspiration and the Interpretation of Sacred Scripture

Paragraph 11 is worth reading and pondering many times in order to draw from it all its many rich ideas.

1. "Those divinely revealed realities which are contained and presented in sacred Scripture have been committed to writing under the inspiration of the Holy Spirit."

Notice that this just states the fact; it does not propose an explanation for "how" this inspiration takes place.

What is your assessment of the explanation of the process of inspiration proposed in this study session?

Do you have an alternative proposal of how the Holy Spirit inspired the human authors of the Bible?

2. Further, the church believes that "the books of the Old and New Testaments *in their entirety,* with all their parts, are sacred and canonical because, having been written under the inspiration of the Holy Spirit they have God as their author."

Reflect on the phrase "in their entirety, with all their parts." Recall the different parts of Proverbs or Ben Sirach that you have read, and imagine that all these parts as well as the entirety of these books have been inspired by the Holy Spirit.

Think of some parts of Proverbs or Sirach that you have read and with which you disagree. How does your agreement or disagreement affect the inspiration of scripture?

If the biblical books you have read are inspired, how can it be that some of their parts might not be at all inspirational or inspiring for you?

The word "canonical" means normative, authoritative. The word "canon" usually describes that entire collection of books in the Bible which are recognized as normative and authoritative. What do you think of the fact that to this day, there is no universal agreement on the contents of the Christian canon of scripture? Protestant Bibles contain fewer books than Catholic Bibles.

3. The Bible makes no mistakes!

> Therefore, since everything asserted by the inspired authors or sacred writers must be held to be asserted by the Holy Spirit, it follows that the books of Scripture must be acknowledged as teaching firmly, faithfully, and *without error that truth which God wanted put into the sacred writings for the sake of our salvation.*

The key words are "truth without error" and "for the sake of our salvation." (par. 11)

This conviction of the church often causes serious problems for many believers who have difficulty believing that texts such as the creation story present "truth without error." What is often left out of the consideration is the other phrase, "for the sake of our salvation."

Utilizing these two phrases in tandem, review what you have learned of the wisdom literature and see if you can identify therein examples of "truth which God wanted" to include "for the sake of our salvation."

Resources

Boadt, Lawrence, C.S.P. *Reading the Old Testament: An Introduction.* New York/Mahwah: Paulist Press, 1984, pp. 11–27.

Collins, Raymond, F. "Inspiration," in *The New Jerome Biblical Commentary.* Englewood Cliffs, N.J.: Prentice-Hall, 1990. #65. pp. 1023–1033.

McBrien, Richard. Chapter VII, "Revelation," in *Catholicism* Vol. 1. Minneapolis, MN.: Winston, 1980, pp. 201–243.

Resources

The two basic resources for this Bible-study program are (1) a Bible and (2) this workbook.

Any Bible translated from the original languages is recommended. It would be especially helpful if the Bible contains cross-references, notes, maps, and other study aids.

For further information about Bible translations consult:

John J. Pilch, *Selecting a Bible Translation,* Collegeville, MN.: The Liturgical Press, 1987.

Paulist Press publishes two excellent handbooks which can readily serve as supplements to this present Bible-study program for those who have the time and may be interested:

Lawrence Boadt, C.S.P., *Reading the Old Testament: An Introduction.* Paulist Press, 1984.

Pheme Perkins, *Reading the New Testament.* Paulist Press, 1985.

Additional helpful information can be found in the following highly recommended books located in many public and parish libraries:

The Collegeville Bible Commentary, Dianne Bergant and Robert J. Karris, eds., Collegeville, MN.: The Liturgical Press, 1988.
A Catholic Commentary by Catholic scholars.

Harper's Bible Commentary, James L. Mays, general editor. San Francisco: Harper and Row, 1988.
An ecumenical commentary by outstanding scholars of various denominations, including Catholics.

Harper's Bible Dictionary, Paul J. Achtemeier, general editor, San Francisco: Harper and Row, 1985.

Insightful and pointed articles on many topics of interest to all Bible readers.

There is much information about Mediterranean culture in atlases of the Bible. Recent publications include the following:

The Harper Atlas of the Bible, James C. Pritchard, editor. San Francisco: Harper & Row, 1987.

Atlas of the Bible, John Rogerson. New York: Facts on File Publications, 1985.

The Zondervan NIV Atlas of the Bible, Carl G. Rasmussen. Grand Rapids, MI.: Zondervan, 1989.

Oxford Bible Atlas, H.G. May, editor. Third Revised Edition, New York: Oxford, 1984.

This last book is also excellent and perhaps the most affordable of those listed for a personal library.